The Big Book of FILTH

With an Introduction by

Jonathon Green

and cartoons by Kipper Williams

CASSELL

First published 1999 by
Cassell
Wellington House
125 Strand
London
WC2R 0BB

First paperback edition 2002
Reprinted 2002

A CIP record for this book is available from the British Library.

ISBN 0 304 36387 1

Distributed in the United States by Sterling Publishing Company Inc.
387 Park Avenue South, New York, NY 10016–8810

Design by Gwyn Lewis

Printed and bound by Aubin, France

The
Big Book
of
FILTH

Contents

best leg of three

Introduction

Filth: Moral defilement, vileness; corruption, pollu-
tion; obscenity. Foul or obscene language; vile or
loathsome imputations.   *OED*

'Arseholes, bastards, fucking cunts and pricks . . .'
Ian Dury 'Plaistow Patricia' (1977)

Ask any cabbie, he knows: yer slang, yer actual slang is
composed of two parts, an' that's yer lot. There's the
rhyming stuff – apples and pears, Gary Glitter, four-by-two
– and then there's the filth. Dirty words, swearing,
obscenity: Mr. Dury's mini-lexicon and much, much more.
He's wrong, the Westminster (*Westminster Abbey* =
cabbie), of course, but he's got an undeniable point. The
slang vocabulary, if my own files are to be trusted, runs to
some 78,000 words and phrases. What you have here,
culled unashamedly from the *Cassell Dictionary of Slang*
(in which they all, irrespective of 'cleanliness', repose), are
around 6,500 of the coarsest, the most lubricious, the
downest and distinctly dirtiest. (Nor are they all listed
here, for even in these singularly degenerate pages there are
areas through which we elected not to pass). Which makes
around eight per cent: in vocabulary terms, a seriously
hefty chunk. Turn to the grand panjandrum of lexicog-
raphy, the *Oxford English Dictionary*, and there's nothing
like so magnificent a presence.

But if slang, as I would suggest, represents the 'counter-language', the spoken opposition to politer tongues, what else would one expect? It covers, in comparison with Standard English, a narrow waterfront, but in enormous depth. Slang scores poorly on abstracts, but it is the concrete terminology that informs the lists that follow. We need this coarse subset, and it doesn't work if you keep it 'proper'. The earliest of all slang 'dictionaries' – the 'canting' glossaries of the 16th century, listing the vocabularies of the underworld – codify not merely the bewildering hierarchy of contemporary criminal beggars, but also have a place for sex. In long-lost doggerel we learn of 'Wapping dell that niggles well' and 'Mort Wap-apace', celebrations of girls who, in today's terms, were 'well up for it'. The parts of the body – *skincoat*, *mutton* and *carnal-trap* for vagina; *rubigo*, *cod* and *poperine pear* for penis – are naturally on display. As are arousal and frustration, the people and places of commercial sex, disease and defecation: the full spectrum of a vocabulary that can be encapsulated as 'filth'. Only 'kinky' sex and homosexuality elude these early compilers – and they will be along in due course.

The nature of slang – even if less so in an age of mass media – is to set aside an area of language (just as its users set aside an area of society) and disguise the terminology within it. The idea that slang, as it was seen to do half a millennium ago, actually bemuses the authorities with its strange circumlocutions, is perhaps a little optimistic. From such early 17th-century playwrights as Middleton and Dekker to the scriptwriters of today's soaps and cop shows, the desire to parade one's 'insider' knowledge has ensured that slang, even if momentarily secret, would soon be available for mass consumption. Never more than today, when slang coiners, consciously or not, must run ever faster to stay on the linguistic cutting edge.

Slang is not all 'dirty words', but if this selection is anything to go by, pretty much all dirty words are slang. 'Filth' these may be, but words they remain: varying aggregations of consonants and vowels. Slang, the great challenger, is thankfully imperishable. Five centuries of impurity and lust are enshrined within; novelties as yet unpenned lie on the tips of unsung tongues. I for one can't wait.

Jonathon Green

kiss the worm

Abbreviations

abbr.	abbreviation	occas.	occasionally
Aus.	Australian	Old Fr.	Old French
Baham.	Bahamas/	orig.	originally
	Bahamian	perh.	perhaps
Bdos.	Barbados/	rhy. sl.	rhyming slang
	Barbadian	S. Afr.	South African
Belz.	Belize	Scot.	Scottish
Can.	Canada/	sl.	slang
	Canadian	Sp.	Spanish
dial.	dialect	teen	teenage use
Eng.	English	Trin.	Trinidad
esp.	especially	Und.	Underworld
ext.	extension	usu.	usually
Ital.	Italian	US	United States
juv.	juvenile (pre-	USVI	United States
	teenage) use		Virgin Islands
lit.	literally	W.I.	West Indies/
N.Z.	New Zealand		West Indian

The terms *Polari*, *Krio* and *Twi* are occasionally used in the text and refer, respectively, to a type of camp slang, to a creole language of Sierra Leone and to a language of southern Ghana.

How to enjoy *The Big Book of Filth*

The Big Book of Filth presents sex slang words and phrases under a variety of categories and headings. Each word or phrase is followed by a date in square brackets, [18C], [19C], [late 18C-early 19C] and so on, indicating the period of usage of the word or phrase in question. The + sign indicates that the term is still in use, as does the label [1990s] which indicates a recent and current expression.

The round brackets that follow the square brackets contain a range of different types of additional information, including usage labels indicating the geographical usage of the word e.g. (US) or the social/cultural usage e.g. (US campus). Where necessary the round brackets also include brief glosses or etymological explanations for some of the more baffling words and phrases.

11

Boys

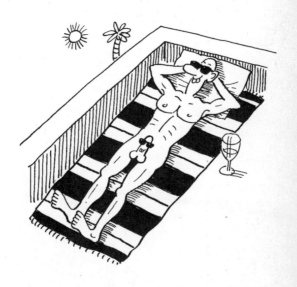

THE GENITALS

accoutrements [19C+]
area [1970s+] (US campus)
arsenal [1990s]
bag of tricks [mid-19C+]
basket [1940s+] (gay)
bat and balls [1940s+] (Aus.)
crown jewels [1960s+]
dongs and gongs [20C] (US gay)
down there [20C]
equipment [1960s+]
family jewels [1960s+]
gear [late 19C+]
genials [1960s+]
goodies [1950s+] (orig. US)
kit [19C+]
luggage [20C]
lunchbox [1990s]
marriage gear [mid-19C+]
naughty bits [1970s+]
necessaries [20C]
packet [1960s+] (orig. gay)
plumbing [1960s+] (orig. US)
private property [20C]
privates [late 18C+]
rhubarb [late 19C+]
rig [1960s+]
rude parts [1970s+]
stock-in-trade [late 19C-1900s]
tackle [20C]

tiddley-hoy [1930s] (Irish)
tiddleypush [1930s] (Irish)
wedding kit [1910s+]
wedding tackle [1910s+]

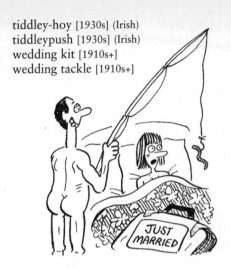

JUST MARRIED

15

THE GENITALS AS A TRIO

barber's sign [late 18C-early 19C]
   ('a standing pole and two washballs')
meat and two veg [1990s]
okra and prunes [1980s]
stick and bangers [late 19C]
string and nuggets [20C]
three-piece set [1970s+]
three-piece suite [1970s+]
watch and seals [mid-19C]

THE TESTICLES

acorns [1970s] (US)
agates [1940s+] (US)
apples [16C+]
apricots [1990s] (Aus.)
back wheels [1990s]
bags [1960s] (US gay)
ballocks [late 18C+]
balls [mid-18C+]
bangers [1980s+] (Irish)
bannocks [1990s]
bat [1940s+] (Aus.)
baubles/bawbles [late 18C-19C]
Beecham's [late 19C+] (i.e. 'pills')
berries [20C] (US Black)
bobbies [19C]
bobbles [late 19C-1920s]
bollockbag [1990s]
boo-boos [1950s] (US)
bulbs [1990s]
bullets [19C]
bum-balls [19C]
callibisters [16C]
cannonballs [19C]
chimes [1960s] (US)
Christ-apples [20C] (US)
chuckies [1990s]
clappers [1930s+]
clinkers [20C] (Ulster)
clock-weights [19C]

16

meat and two veg

cobs [19C]
cods [19C+]
cojones [1920s+]
conkers [1990s]
crab on the rocks [late 19C] (i.e. itching testicles)
cullions [16C]
culls [16C-17C]
danglers [mid-19C+]
diamonds [1960s] (US gay)
ding-dongs [1950s+] (US)
dowsetts [17C] (*dowset* = a deer's testicles)
dusters [1950s] (i.e. they hang so low that they 'dust'
   the floor)
eggs [1950s+] (US)
eggs in the basket [1960s] (US gay)
frick and frack [1980s+] (US Black; from the imagined
   sound of their knocking together)
gingambobs [late 18C-19C]
glands [1910s-20s] (US)
goatees [1960s] (US gay)
gonads [1910s+] (US)
gongs [1950s] (US gay)
gonicles [1950s] (US)
goolies [1930s+] (Aus.)
gooseberries [20C]
happy sack [1990s]
jelly bag [17C]
jizzbags [1990s]
kaks [20C] (Irish)
kanakas [20C] (Aus.)
knackers [mid-19C+]

knacks [mid-19C+]
nackers [mid-19C+]
knockers [late 19C+]
love apples [19C; 1980s+]
love spuds [1990s]
male-mules [16C]
marbles [mid-19C+]
nackers [mid-19C+]
nadgers [1950s+]
nads [1960s+] (orig. US)
nags [late 17C-mid-18C]
nerts [1930s] (US)
nick-nacks [18C-19C]
noogies [1980s] (US)
nutmegs [late 17C-early 19C]
nuts [mid-19C+]
orbs [1960s] (US gay)
pebbles [19C]
pills [late 19C+]
plums [20C]
pounders [17C]
rocks [1940s+]
rollies [1930s+]
scalloped potatoes [1960s] (US gay)
seals [mid-19C]
slabs [20C]
slashers [1960s]
swingers [19C]
tallywags/tarrywags [late 18C-early 19C]
taws [20C] (Irish)

thingumabobs/thingumbobs [mid-18C+]
thingummies [early 19C+]
twiddle-diddles [late 18C-early 19C]
velvet orbs [1960s] (US gay)
whiblin [early-mid-17C]
whirligigs [late 17C-early 19C]
yarbles [1970s+]
yongles/yoongles [1990s]

crab on the rocks

THE TESTICLES IN RHYMING SLANG

rhyming with *bollocks*
betty swallocks [1990s] ('sweaty bollocks')
fun and frolics [1940s-60s]
flowers and frolics [1940s-60s]
jimmy rollocks [20C]
Sandra Bullocks [1990s]
tommy rollocks [20C]

rhyming with *balls*
cobblers [1930s+]
cobblers' awls [1930s+]
cobblers' stalls [1930s+]
coffee stalls [1940s-60s]
Henry Halls [1950s+]
marble halls [20C]
Max Walls [1950s+]
Niagara Falls [1960s+]
nobby halls [20C]
orchestra stalls [20C]
Wentworth Falls [1920s+] (Aus.)
Wentworth's balls [1920s+] (Aus.)

rhyming with *knackers*
Christmas crackers [1970s+]
cream crackers [1940s-60s]

rhyming with *nuts*
General Smuts [20C]

rhyming with *cods*
Ken Dodds [20C]

rhyming with *goolies*
Tom Doolies [1950s]

THE SCROTUM

bag [late 19C-1930s]
ball-bag [19C+]
ballbasket [1960s+]
bo-dick [1990s] (US Black)
bo-jack [1990s] (US Black)
bollockbag [1990s]
bozack/'zack [1990s] (orig. US Black teen)
daddy-bag [1990s] (US Black)
grand bag [1970s] (gay)
nadbag [1990s]
nutsack [1970s+] (US)
purse [late 17C-18C]
raisin bag [1990s] (Can.)
sack o' nuts [1970s] (US Black)
tadpole carrier [1990s]
winkybag [1990s]

21

nutsack

THE PENIS

THE MEMBER

dearest member [19C]
fornicating member [19C]
hot lot/member [19C-1910s] (US)
jolly member [19C]
limb [11C-late 19C]
master member [19C]
member for cockshire [mid-19C]

THE WEAPON

Adam's whip [1950s] (US)
arse-opener [19C+]
arse-wedge [19C]
battering piece [19C]
beard-splitter [late 17C-early 18C]
belly-ruffian [late 17C-18C]
bingey [late 19C] (dial. *bing* = to hit)
blue-veined custard chucker [1990s]
bow [17C] (it 'fires arrows')
bush-beater [19C]
bush-whacker [20C]
cherry splitter [19C]
chopper [20C]
cock-opener [1920s-40s] (US Black; *cock* = vagina)
cracker [19C]
diddlywhacker [1960s] (US)
dillywhacker [1920s] (US)

ding-dong [1940s+] (US)
dingbat [1910s-40s]
dinger [1950s] (US)
dong [20C] (orig. US)
donger [20C] (Aus.)
hair-divider [20C]
hair-splitter [20C]
instrument [late 16C-17C]
jammy [1980s+] (US Black)
knock [18C+]
lance [late 16C-early 17C]
love truncheon [1990s]
nudger [1960s] (US)
plonker [1960s+]
plug-tail [late 18C-mid-19C]
poll-axe [19C]
power [mid-19C+]
purple-headed custard chucker [1970s+]
purple-headed love truncheon [1970s+]
quimstake [17C]
quimwedge [17C]
rump-splitter [19C]
salty yogurt slinger [1990s]
sexing-piece [1920s+]
split rump [19C]
striker [19C]
swack [1970s+] (US Black)
swipe [1950s-70s] (US Black)
sword [late 16C-early 17C]
thrumster [late 17C-early 19C]
twanger [late 16C-late 19C]

wang [1930s+] (orig. US)
wanger [1930s+] (orig. US)
wang-tang [1970s+] (US Black)
weapon [early 11C+]
whammer [20C]
whang [1930s+] (orig US)
whangdoodle/wangdoodle/wingdoodle [1970s+] (US)
whanger [1930s+]
wong [1980s+]
yang [20C]
ying-yang [1960s+]

THE DISTURBER

24

bum-tickler [18C]
enemy [19C]
claw-buttock [19C]
eye opener [19C]
girl-catcher [19C]
girlometer [mid-late 19C]
impudence [mid-18C-late 19C]
jumble-giblets [17C]
leather dresser [19C]
leather-stretcher [19C]
lung-disturber [20C]
pillicock [early 14C-early 18C]
placket-racket [17C] (*placket* = prostitute)
plum tree shaker [17C]
tickle faggot [19C]
tickle-gizzard [19C]
tickle-tail [late 15C-late 18C]

tickle-toby [late 17C-19C]
trouble-giblets [18C]
tummy tickler [mid-late 19C]

THE KNIFE

Adam's dagger [late 18C]
bayonet [19C]
beaver cleaver [1990s]
beef bayonet [1960s+]
blade [late 19C]
bodkin [19C]
butcher knife [1980s+]
butter-knife [19C]
cutlass [17C]
cutty gun [19C]
dagger [19C]
dard [17C-18C] (i.e. 'a dart')
dirk [18C; 1960s]
dobber [1970s] (US)
harpoon [20C]
lance of love [19C]
love-dart [19C]
mutton bayonet [1990s]
mutton dagger [1960s+]
needle [mid-17C-mid-18C; 1930s-60s]
pike [19C]
pikestaff [late 18C-1900s]
pin [late 17C+]
pintle [early 18C-19C]
pork sword [1960s+]

prick [late 16C+]
samurai sword [1980s+]
shit-stabber [1960s+]
sting [late 19C]
tosh [late 19C] (i.e. 'a tusk')

THE GUN

bacon bazooka [1990s]
banger [20C]
bazooka [1950s+]
blue-veined porridge gun [1990s]
blue-veined yoghurt gun [1990s]
cannon [1960s-70s] (US)
cock [early 17C+]
gun [late 17C; 19C+]
heat-seeking missile [1990s] (US campus)
hogleg [1940s] (nickname of the Colt .45)
lamb cannon [1990s]
loaded gun [1980s+]
love gun [1970s+] (US)
love torpedo [1990s]
moisture missile [1990s]
musket [1930s-70s] (US)
mutton gun [1940s-50s]
mutton musket [1990s]
peacemaker [1970s] (US Black)
pillicock pistol [early 18C]
pistol [late 16C+]
porridge gun [1990s]
portable pocket rocket [1990s]

sexocet missile [1990s]
shooting iron [19C] (US)
shooting stick [19C]
sticky spud gun [1990s]
trouser mauser [1990s]
winny-popper [1950s+] (Can. juv.)

THE STICK

bamboo [1970s] (W.I.)
bat [1940s+] (Aus.)
blow-stick [1960s+]
broom-handle [19C]
clothes-prop [19C]
copper-stick [19C]
coral branch [19C]
dibble [19C] (i.e. a garden 'drill')
drumstick [19C-1900s]
fiddlestick [late 16C-early 17C]
fiddling-stick [19C]
flesh pencil [1990s]
fuckpole [1990s]
fuckstick [1960s+]
gigglestick [20C] (US)
giggling-pin [20C] (US)
glory pole [1950s] (US)
gulley raker [19C]
gutstick [1970s] (US Black)
handstaff [mid-19C+]
jolly stick [1970s] (US Black)
joy prong [1910s-70s]

kennel raker [19C]
langer [1980s+] (Irish; i.e. 'a long one')
love stick [1920s+] (US)
magic wand [1960s]
night stick [1910s+] (US)
passion stick [1950s] (Aus.)
pile-driver [19C]
pilgrim's staff [18C]
pipe [1960s+]
ploughshare [19C]
pole [19C+]
prod [late 19C+]
prong [1960s+]
pronger [1960s+]
ramrod [19C]
reamer [1970s+]
rod [20C]
rolling-pin [mid-late 19C]
roly-poly [19C]
sceptre [19C]
sensitive truncheon [19C]
shitstick [1960s+]
shove-straight [18C]
spike-faggot [17C] (*faggot* = woman)
spindle [19C]
staff of life [19C]
stick [17C+]
tentpeg [19C]
truncheon [19C]
tube [1920s]
veiny bang-stick [1990s]

wand [19C]
whore-pipe [late 18C-19C]
wood [19C+]
wriggling pole [18C]
wriggling stick [18C]
yard [19C] (orig. 'a thin pole')

SWEETIES

blue-veined junket pump [1990s]
candy cane [late 19C-1960s]
cinnamon stick [1940s-60s]
creamstick [19C+]
cremorne [19C] (i.e. 'cream horn')
dolly [19C]
gobstopper [20C]
ice-cream machine [20C]
jelly [1920s+] (US Black)
ladies' lollipop [19C]
lollipop [19C; 1960s+]
popsicle [1980s+]
pud [1930s+]
pudding [late 17C+]
stick of rock [20C]
sugarstick [late 18C-1900s]
sweetmeat [1980s+]
tit-bit [mid-17C-late 18C]
yum-yum [late 19C+]

FRUIT AND VEG

banana [1910s+]
bean [late 19C-1900s]
bean-tosser [19C]
carrot [19C]
cob [1920s-60s] (US)
cucumber [late 19C+] (US)
fruit for the monkeys [1950s+]
goober [1920s+] (US; i.e. 'a peanut')
lunch [1940s+]
noodle [1970s+] (US Black)
okra [1920s-50s] (US)
pickle [20C] (orig US)
poperine pear [late 16C] (punning on 'pop her in')
potato-finger [17C]
string bean [1970s]
    (US Black; 'a long thin penis')
tummy banana [1980s+]

THE PENIS AS A FISH

cod [late 18C+]
crab ladder [1990s]
    (*crab* = pubic louse)
eel [1960s+]
one-eyed zipper fish [1990s]
trouser trout [20C] (US)
zipperfish [1990s]

THE BUTCHER'S SHOP

bacon [1910s-20s]
baloney [20C] (orig US)
beef [early 19C+]
blue-veined steak [1980s+]
bone [1910s+]
bone phone [20C] (US)
burrito [1980s+] (US campus)
butcher [19C]
chitterling [19C]
crimson chitterling [19C]
dark meat [late 19C+]
enchilada [1970s] (US)
goose's neck [late 19C]
gravy-giver [19C] (*gravy* = semen)
gristle [19C]
hairy sausage [1990s]
ham howitzer [1990s]
hambone [20C]
hogger [1980s+] (US)
hot dog [1920s+]
knockwurst [1970s] (US)
live rabbit [19C]
live sausage [19C]
lizard [1960s+] (Aus./US)
lovesteak [1980s+] (US campus)
marrow-pudding [mid-19C]
marrowbone and cleaver [mid-19C]
meat [late 16C-18C; 20C]
meat axe [1970s]

meat-cleaver [20C]
meat lance [1970s+] (US)
meat puppet [1990s] (US)
meat spear [1970s+] (US)
meat stick [1970s+] (US)
meat tool [1960s+] (US)
meat whistle [1940s+] (US)
mutton [late 16C]
pussy fodder [1990s]
raw meat [late 18C+]
rooster [19C+] (US Black)
sausage [19C+]
schnitzel [1950s+]
snorker [1940s+] (Aus.; i.e. 'a sausage')
spam javelin [1990s]
split mutton [17C-19C]
tubesteak [1960s+] (US)
turkey neck [1950s+]

NAMES AND PERSONIFICATIONS

Abraham [19C]
bald-headed hermit [late 19C+]
Barney [1970s] (US Black)
Bluebeard [19C]
Blueskin [19C]
bo-dick [1990s] (US Black)
bo-jack [1990s] (US Black)
the boy [late 19C+]
boyo [late 19C+]
buddy [1980s+] (US)

THE PENIS IN RHYMING SLANG: PART 1

rhyming with *prick* or *dick*
- bob and dick [1970s]
- donkey/donkey's [20C]
- gigglestick [20C] (US)
- Hampton Wick [late 19C+]
- joystick [1910s+] (orig US)
- kiss-me-quick [20C]
- mad Mick [20C] (Aus.)
- moby dick [late-19C+]
- Pat and Mick [late 19C+]
- pogo/pogo stick [1970s+] (Aus.)
- stormy Dick [20C] (US)
- sugar-stick [20C] (US)
- Uncle Dick [1970s+]

rhyming with *cock*
- almond/almond rock [late 19C+]
- dickery/dickory dock [late 19C+]
- grandfather/grandfather clock [20C]
- Hampton rock [late 19C+]
- padlock [1960s-70s]
- stick of rock [20C]

Captain Standish [18C] ('he always stands for a lady')
charley/charlie [1960s]
Comrade Wobbly [1990s] (mainly upper-middle class)
D [1990s] (US Black; *D* = dick)

THE PENIS IN RHYMING SLANG: PART 2

rhyming with *penis*
good ship Venus [20C]
Mars and Venus [20C]
rhyming with *horn*
Marquis of Lorne
[mid-19C]
rhyming with *tadger*
fox and badger [1990s]
rhyming with *bean*
haricot [late 19C-1900s]
rhyming with *chopper*
gobstopper [20C]
rhyming with *knob*
Uncle Bob

dick [late 19C+]
Don Cypriano [17C] (*Cyprian* = whore)
Dr Johnson [19C] ('he stood up to anyone')
Fagan/Fagin [1950s]
Herman the One-eyed German [1990s] (US campus)
J.T. [mid-19C+] (i.e. '*John Thomas*')
jack [19C+]
Jack in the box [late 19C+]
Jack Robinson [19C]
Jacob [19C] (it 'climbs' the vagina's 'ladder')
Jezabel [19C]
jimbrowsky/jim browski [1980s+] (US Black)

jimmy [1980s+]
jock [late 18C+]
john [1910s+]
John Henry [late 19C+]
John Thomas [mid-19C+] (*John Thomas* originally
    meant 'servant', thus he 'stands' in the presence of a lady)
John Willie [19C]
johnnie/johnny [1930s+]
jojo [1960s+] (US Black)
jones [1960s+] (US Black)
Julius Caesar [19C]
lad [20C] (Irish)
the law [1970s+] (US Black)
little brother [mid-19C+] (US Black)
little Davy [17C+]
little man [20C]
long dong silver [1980s] (US)
long tom [late 19C]
man Thomas [early 17C-early 19C]
Master John Goodfellow [19C]
Master John Thursday [19C]
mickey [20C] (Irish)
Moby Dick [late-19C+]
Mr Happy Helmet [1990s]
Mr Peaslin [19C] (*pizzle* = bull's penis)
old blind bob [18C]
old boy [1940s+] (US)
old fellow [early 19C+]
Old Hornie/Horney [20C]
Old Hornington [19C]
old man [late 19C+]

old Slimey [18C]
old soldier [1970s] (US)
old thing [1970s+]
one-eyed brother [1990s] (US Black)
Percy [1960s+]
Peter [late 19C+]
Polyphemus [19C] (the 'one-eyed monster')
putz [1930s+] (Yiddish)
red cap [1910s+]
Robin [mid-late 19C+]
Roger [late 17C+]
scallywag/scallawag [1990s] (US)
schmuck [20C] (German 'ornament')
Sir John [late 19C]
Sir Martin Wagstaffe [mid-17C]
St Peter [19C] (he 'keeps the keys of Paradise')
Thomas [mid-19C+]
Tom [mid-late 19C]
William [mid-19C+]
Wyatt Earp [1970s] (the famous 'gunman')
yutz [20C] (Yiddish)

THE JOB-HOLDER

ambassador [1920s] (US)
buttonhole worker [19C]
corporal [20C] (US)
corporal love [20C] (US)
customs officer [late 18C] (he works in the *custom house*, i.e. vagina)
foreman [19C]

general [1960s] (US)
gentleman usher [late 16C-early 17C]
milkman [1990s]
ranger [17C-18C]
rector of the females [17C]
solicitor general [19C]
tinker [1950s-60s]
vestryman [19C]

NURSERY TERMS

dicky [late 19C+]
doodle [late 18C+]
peenie [20C]
peewee [19C]
tinkle [1930s+]
weenie [1910s+] (usu. US juv.)
wienie [1910s+] (usu. US juv.)
willy [20C]
winkle [1940s+]
winky [late 19C+]

THE SHAPE

blue-veined havana [1990s]
bobby-dangler [1930s+]
button [19C+]
crank [1960s+] (orig. US)
dangler [1930s-50s]
derrick [19C]
dingle-dangle [late 19C+]

doodle-flap [late 19C]
drop [1950s] (Aus.)
flapdoodle [17C]
flapper [17C]
flip-flap [mid-17C]
floater [19C]
hanging johnny [19C]
hang-out [1980s+]
inch [19C]
nubbin [1930s+] (US Black)
obelisk [19C]
pen [late 16C-1900s]
pendulum [19C]
pimple [late 19C+]
shaft [late 18C+]
shaft of delight [mid-18C]
spigot [19C]
yoyo [20C] (US; it goes 'up and down')

THE INSTRUMENT OF INTERCOURSE

do-jigger [1960s+]
driving post [1960s+]
fornicator [19C]
jigger [mid-19C]
jiggling bone [19C]
joint [1930s+] (US; it 'joins' the partners)
tadger [late 19C+] (northern UK dial.; *tadge* = stitch together)
todger [late 19C+]

THE BURROWER

chutney ferret [1970s+]
crack-haunter [19C]
crack-hunter [19C]
cranny-haunter [19C]
cunny-burrow ferret [17C]
cunny-catcher [17C]
ferret [late 19C+]
maggot [20C]
mole [late 19C-1910s]
mouldiworp [1990s]
mouse [19C]

THE MUSICAL INSTRUMENT

bell rope [1960s-70s] (US)
blue-veined piccolo [1980s+]
blue-veined trumpet [1980s+]
ding [1960s-70s]
dingaling [1950s+] (orig. US Black)
family organ [1920s-50s] (US)
fiddle-bow [19C]
fleshy flugelhorn [1990s]
flute [19C+]
gospel-pipe [1910s-20s] (US)
honk [1960s-70s] (US)
honker [1970s+]
horn [late 18C+]
kazoo [1960s+]
living flute [19C+]

lute [19C]
oboe [1990s]
pink oboe [1990s]
silent flute [19C+]
skin flute [19C+]
ting-a-ling [1900s] (US Black)
trouser trumpet [1990s]
whistle [late 19C]

THE ENGINE

engine [mid-late 18C]
fornicating engine [19C]
garden engine [19C]
gaying instrument [18C]
love machine [1960s+]
love pump [1980s+] (US)
machine [mid-18C; 1950s+]
pink bus [1990s]

THE TOOL

auger [1900s-10s]
ax [1910s-60s] (US)
beeze [1940s] (*bezel* = cutting tool)
bowsprit [mid-18C+]
bridle-string [late 19C]
broomstick [19C]
cleat [late 19C]
coupling bat [20C]
coupling pin [1910s] (US)

crowbar [1920s] (US)
dipstick [1960s+] (orig US)
drill [1910s-20s] (US)
driving post [20C]
flange [20C]
fornicating tool [19C]
gadget/gidget [1940s+] (US)
gaff [1960s] (US)
generation tool [19C]
gimmick [1960s] (US)
gizmo/gismo [1940s+] (US)
grinding tool [19C]
hammer-handle [1920s-50s] (US)
hammerhead [1990s]
handle [1960s+] (US)
hoe-handle [1920s-50s] (US)
holy poker [mid-19C+]
hose [1920s+] (US)
iron [late 17C-early 18C; 1930s+]
joystick [1910s+] (orig US)
kit [19C]
knob [mid-17C; 1920s+]
joy knob [1950s+] (US)
lanyard [1990s]
nature's scythe [19C]
nob [early 19C+]
nozzle [1990s] (US)
padlock [1960s-70s]
piston [20C]
plunger [1930s+]
pointer [late 19C+]

41

poker [early 19C]
pump [18C-late 19C]
pump-handle [18C-late 19C]
rammer [late 18C-19C]
red-hot poker [late 19C+]
rogering iron [18C-19C]
rudder [19C]
screwdriver [20C]
seal [mid-17C]
shunter's pole [20C]
sternpost [mid-late 19C]
string [1950s+] (US)
tool [mid-19C+]
wedge [mid-19C]
wick [20C]
wire [20C]

HORTICULTURAL

acorn [19C]
bog bamboo [1970s+]
gardener [mid-19C]
Irish root [19C]
lily [1940s+] (US)
log [1970s+] (US)
lumber [1970s+] (US)
man root [19C]
old root [19C]
pego [late 17C-late 19C] (Greek 'fountain')
pioneer of nature [19C]
root [mid-19C+]

sensitive plant [early-mid-19C]
tail [late 17C-early 18C]
veiny love-stalk [1990s]

ZOOLOGICAL

bird [late 19C+]
birdie [20C]
chanticleer [mid-late 19C] (lit. 'cockerel')
cock-robin [1970s]
cockerel [mid-late 17C]
cuckoo [19C]
dicky-bird [1950s]
dinosaur [1980s+] (US Black)
dog [20C] (US)
donkey [20C]
dragon [1980s+] (US)
earthworm [1990s]
fang [1950s+]
fanny rat [1990s]
hog [1960s+] (US)
jimmy dog [20C]
Master Reynard [19C] (*Reynard* = fox)
monkey [1980s+] (US campus)
mud snake [1990s] (US; from the expression *mud for one's
    turtle*, meaning sex from the man's point of view)
mule [1940s+] (US)
nags [late 17C-mid-18C]
one-eyed cyclops [1990s]
one-eyed monster [1960s] (US)
one-eyed stag [late 18C]

43

one-eyed trouser snake
    [1960s+] (orig. Aus.)
pecker [late 19C+] (orig. US)
pizzle [1960s] (Aus.; lit. 'bull's penis')
poodle [1920s-50s] (US)
poodle-dink [1920s-50s] (US)
purple ridgeback [1990s]
rabbit [19C]
schlong [1930s+] (Yiddish. 'snake')
slug [1940s+] (orig. Aus. navy)
snake [1960s+] (US)
toad [1980s+] (US)
weasel [1980s+] (orig. US)
woofer [1980s+] (US)
worm [1980s+]

ANATOMICAL

arm [1970s+]
bald-headed bandit [1960s+]
bald-headed champ [late 19C+]
bald-headed friar [late 19C+]
bald-headed sailor [late 19C+]
best leg of three [late 19C-1900s]
big foot Joe [20C]
fuck muscle [1980s+] (US gay)

hang-down [20C]
love arm [1990s]
love bone [1960s+] (US Black)
man muscle [1970s+] (US Black)
middle finger [late 19C+]
middle leg [late 19C+]
pigtail [20C]
pinkler [late 19C+] (refers to its fleshy pinkness)
purple-headed avenger/p.h.a. [1990s]
purple-headed monster [1970s+]
schwantz [20C] (US; Yiddish 'tail')
short arm [20C]
stump [20C]
tallywag [18C] (lit. 'wagging tail')
tallywagger [18C]
tallywhacker [18C]
third leg [1970s+]
thumb of love [20C]

EUPHEMISTIC

Aaron's Rod [19C]
Adam's Arsenal [19C]
affair [mid-19C]
arbor vitae [18C] (Latin 'tree of life')
athenaeum [late 19C-1900s] (a pun on 'club')
big one [1990s]
concern [19C]
Cupid's torch [19C]
dingo [1970s] (US)
dingus [19C+] (i.e. 'thingumibob')

dingwallace [1920s] (US)
dinky [1980s+]
end [1910s+]
Father Abraham [19C]
father confessor [19C]
father-of-all [19C]
flim-flam [1970s] (US; lit. 'a trifle')
he [19C+]

THE DEFECATORY PENIS

nippy [mid-19C]
pee-pee [1920s+]
pisser [20C]
pooper [1950s+]

46

hobo [1910s] (US; lit. 'a tramp')
it [mid-19C+]
knack [19C]
my body's captain [19C]
old Adam [19C+]
piece [1930s+] (orig. US)
private property [20C]
privates [late 18C+]
she [1920s+] ('up *she* rises')
tantrum [late 17C-late 18C] (dial. *tantril*, 'a wanderer')
that [19C]
that the Lord knows what [19C]

that thing [1900s-40s] (US Black)
thing [1950s+]
thingummy [late 18C+]
toy [19C]
trifle [19C]
what's its name [late 19C]
you know where [20C]

THE WIFE'S BEST FRIEND

baby maker [late 19C-1900s]
bit of snug [late 19C] (lit. 'a cuddle')
brat-getter [19C]
child-getter [19C]
good time [1960s+]

THE BLACK PENIS

black jack [1950s+]
blackleg [20C]
black pencil [1970s]
black pudding [20C]
Jackie Robinson [1960s]
jungle meat [1960s+] (gay)
liquorice/licorice stick [1980s+] (US gay)
midnight lace [1980s+]
sooty jimmy [1980s+] (US Black)

happy lamp [1990s]
ladies' delight [19C]
ladies' plaything [19C]
ladies' treasure [19C]
lady ware [19C]
lamp of light [19C]
lullaby [mid-late 19C] ('it puts one to sleep')
master of ceremonies [19C]
matrimonial peacemaker [late 18C-early 19C]
merrymaker [19C]
partner [19C]
sex [1930s+]
wife's best friend [20C]

48 THE UNCATEGORISABLE PENIS

choad [1960s+] (orig. US high school; Navajo *chodis*, penis)
doob [1950s+] (Aus.)
gooter [1980s+] (Irish)
I.D. [1950s+] (US; puns on 'Let's see your I.D.')
jamoke [1960s] (US)
jock-piece [1920s] (US)
jockum/jockam [16C]
jocky [late 17C+]
reltney [20C] (US)
wooter [1960s] (US)

THE ERECT PENIS

bar [1980s+]
Bethlehem steel [1970s] (US Black; pun on the name
    of a US steel manufacturer)
bit of hard [19C]
bit of stiff [19C]
blue-veined root-on [1990s]
blue vein/veiner [late 19C+]
bone [1910s+]
boner [1960s+]
Britannia metal [19C]
broom-handle [19C]
bugle [1980s+] (Irish)
chubby [1990s]
clothes-prop [19C]
cockstand [mid-19C+]
crouton [1990s] (rhy. sl. 'root-on')
English sentry [1960s+] (US gay)
fat [1930s+] (Aus./N.Z.)
fixed bayonet [19C]
flag [1960s] (US)
guided missile [1970s+] (US Black)
hard [late 19C+]
hard bit [20C]
hard mouthful [20C]
hard-on [late 19C+]
hard up [1930s]
head [1950s+] (US)
horn [late 18C+]
horn colic [late 18C-1950s] (an involuntary erection)

THE ERECT PENIS IN RHYMING SLANG

rhyming with *bone*
full-blown Stallone [1990s]
rhyming with *horn*
colleen bawn [19C]
hail smiling morn [1970s+]
Marquis of Lorne/marquis [1960s+]
mountains of Mourne [20C]
September morn [1970s+]
Sunday morn [20C]
rhyming with *erection*
general election [20C]

hornification [late 18C+]
Irish inch [1970s-80s] (US)
Irish toothache/i.t.a. [19C]
Irish toothpick [1920s] (US)
jack [19C]
jackhammer [1980s+] (US gay)
lance in rest [late 16C-early 17C]
lob/lobb [18C+] (a half- or fully erect penis)
morning pride [late 19C]
morning wood [1990s] (US)
the old man has his Sunday clothes on [19C]
paddy's toothache [19C]
panhandle [1990s]
pink steel [1990s]
popcorn [20C] (rhy. sl. 'horn')

prick-pride [20C]
pride of the morning [late 19C]
prong-on [1960s+]
prong/pronger [1960s+]
rajah [1940s+] (N.Z.)
rise [1940s+]
roaring horn [late 19C] (Aus.)
roaring jack [late 19C] (Aus.)
rod [20C]
root [late 19C+]
root-on [1990s]
scope [1960s+] (i.e. a telescope)
silly [1970s] (N.Z. juv.)
spike [20C]
stalk [late 16C+]
stand [mid-19C-1900s]
standing ware [mid-late 19C]
stand-on [1940s-50s]
star-gazer [17C-18C]
stiff [17C+]
stiff and stout [19C]
stiff deity [19C]
stiffie [1980s+]
stonker [1980s+]
touch-on [1940s+]
wood [1980s+]
wooden spoon [1920s+]
woodie/woody [1990s] (US)
woodrow [1990s]
Yasser Crack-a-fat [1990s] (US)

51

THE FORESKIN

curtains [1980s+] (US gay)
draw drapes [1950s-60s]
goat skin [1960s+] (US gay)
lace [1960s+] (US gay)
lace curtain/curtains [1960s+]
onion skin [1960s+] (US gay)
opera cape [1960s+] (US gay)
snapper [1930s+] (US)

THE HEAD OF THE PENIS

bombhead [1990s]
bell end [1990s]
cock collar [1960s] (US Black)
knob-end [1920s+]
knot [mid-late 19C]

THE GLANS PENIS

bobby's helmet [1930s+]
bobby's hat [1930s+]
cheese ridge [1990s] (the part of the penis between the glans
    and the shaft)
German helmet [1950s+]
helmet [1950s+]
Kojak's rollneck [1990s]
policeman's helmet [1930s+]

THE URETHRA

cheese tube [1990s]
hog-eye/hog's eye [1990s]
Jap's eye [1990s]

THE FRENUM

banjo string [1990s]
bobstay [late 18C+]
bridle string [late 19C]
dickstring [1960s+] (US Black)
throat [20C] (it 'links the head to the body')

policeman's helmet

THE LARGE PENIS

big bird [1960s+]
donkey dick [1970s+]
four-eleven-forty-four [1960s+] (US Black; i.e. 4" thick,
    11" long)
honker [1970s+]
horsecock [1940s+]
horsemeat [1980s+] (US gay)
Jewish compliment [mid-19C+] ('no money but a big
    penis')
kidney-buster [1930s]
kidney-prodder [1960s]
kidney-wiper [late 19C-1960s] (US)
liver-disturber [late 19C]
liver-lifter [late 19C]
lobcock [late 18C+] (a large flaccid penis)
nine-inch knocker [20C]
packing [1990s] (US Black; i.e. it 'packs' the vagina)
sky-scraper [20C]
sollicker [1940s-50s] (lit. 'forcer')
stretcher [mid-18C]

THE SMALL PENIS

bugfucker [1970s] (US)
diddler [19C]
dink [20C] (US)
itty bitty meat/i.b.m. [1960s+] (US)
needle dick [1960s+] (US)
peedie [20C] (Ulster)
pee-wee [19C]
pencil [1930s+]
pencil dick [1980s+] (US)
puppy [1980s+] (US Black)
small meat [1960s+] (US gay)
snack [1990s]
tiddler [19C+]
winky/winkie [late 19C+]

HUNG LIKE A . . .

hung like a bull [1960s+]
hung like a horse [1960s+]
hung like a jack donkey [1960s+]
hung like a mouse/fieldmouse [1960s+]
hung like a mule [1960s+]
hung like a show dog [1960s+]
hung like a stallion [1960s+]
hung like a stud [1960s+]
hung like a stud mosquito [1960s+] (US)
hung low [1990s] (US black)

THE IMPOTENT PENIS

brewer's droop [1970s+] (orig. Aus.)
dead rabbit [20C]
dropping member [19C]
fire blanks [1950s+] (said of an impotent man or of one
    who has had a vasectomy)
Hanging Johnny [19C]
Irish horse [1950s+] (gay)
muddy waters [1970s+] (US Black; the loss of erection
    during sex)

THE IMPOTENT MAN

broken arrow [1960s] (US)
bungler [late 17C-18C]
dominie do-little [late 18C-
    early 19C]
dry balls [1930s-40s] (US)
flapper [19C]
fuck-beggar [18C]
fumbler [late 17C-18C]
fumbler's hall
    [late 17C-early 18C]
    (a place where impotent
    men might be punished
    for their failings)
jaffa [1990s] (i.e. 'seedless')
mule [1950s+] (W.I.)

THE CIRCUMCISED PENIS

clipped [1940s+] (US)
cut joint [1970s+] (US gay)
Jew's/Jewish compliment [1950s-70s] (gay)
Jew's lance [20C]
Jewish corned beef [1960s] (US)
Jewish National [1950s+] (US gay)
kosher dill [1960s+] (US gay)
lop cock [1930s-40s] (US)
low neck and short sleeves [1960s+] (US)
one-eyed boy with his shirtsleeves rolled up
    [1960s+]
ringbarked [1980s+] (N.Z.)
roundhead [20C]

THE UNCIRCUMCISED PENIS

blind [1920s+] (gay)
blind cock [1980s+] (US gay)
blind meat [1920s+] (US gay)
Canadian bacon [1960s+] (gay)
cavalier [20C]
near-sighted [1920s+] (gay)
skin boy [1980s] (N.Z.)
turtleneck [1990s] (US gay)
u/c [1970s+] ('uncut')
wink [1980s+] (US gay)

SEMEN

axle grease [20C]
bip [1990s] (Can.)
bullet [1960s] (US)
chism [late 19C+] (orig. US)
cock puke [1990s]
cock snot [1990s]
come [1920s+]
comings [mid-19C+]
crud/krud [1950s+]
crunt [1950s-60s] (US Black; refers to dried semen)
cum [1920s+]
cundy [1990s] (the post-coital mix of semen and
    vaginal secretions)
dicksplash [1990s]
dog water [1960s+] (US)
face cream [1980s+] (US gay)
fetch [19C] (i.e. that which is 'fetched' or drawn forth)
gism/gissum/gizm/gizzum/gizzem/gyzm [late 19C+]
    (orig. US)
glue [late 19C]
goo [20C] (orig. US)
goo-goo [20C] (orig. US)
Irish confetti [20C] (gay)
jazz [1930s] (US)
jism/jism/jizzum/jiz/jizz [late 19C+] (orig. US)
jit [1970s] (US campus; the 'jet' of an ejaculation)
joombye [1990s] (Scot.)
lather [19C-1900s]
letchwater [19C]

load [1920s+] (US)
lump [late 19C-1920s] (US)
map of England/Ireland [1960s+] (a semen stain on a sheet)
mess [1990s]
mettle [late 18C-early 19C]
milt [19C]
muck [1990s]
ointment [late 18C-late 19C]
paste [1980s+]
pearl [1980s+] (US gay)
pearly passion potion [1990s]
pecker snot [1990s] (US)
population paste [1980s+]
scum [1960s+] (US)

map of England

slime [19C+]
snot [1980s+]
snowball [1990s]
spence [20C] (W.I.; lit. 'spendings')
spend [late 19C]
spew [1980s+] (US campus)
splooge [1980s+] (US campus)
spoo [1980s+] (US campus)
spooch [1980s+] (US campus)
spoof [1910s+] (Aus.)
spooge [1990s] (US)
spratz [1980s+] (US; German *spritzen*, to spray)
spudwater [1990s]
spuff [1990s]
spume [1990s]
spunk [late 19C+]
tallow [19C]
wad [20C]
white swallow [1990s] (US, mainly West Coast)

SEMEN À LA CARTE

baby gravy [1990s]
batter [1990s]
beef gravy [1980s+] (US gay)
bollock yoghurt [1990s]
butter [late 19C+]
cocoa [1970s+]
come-juice [20C]
cream [late 19C+]
creamed beef [1990s]

SEMEN IN RHYMING SLANG

rhyming with *spunk*
Harry Monk [20C]
Maria Monk [late 19C+]
pineapple chunk [1990s] (Scot.)
Thelonius Monk [20C]
Victoria Monk [late 19C-1900s]

rhyming with *come*
Pedigree Chum [1960s+]

custard [1950s] (Aus.)
dick drink [1980s+] (US gay)
duck butter [1930s+] (US)
French dressing [1950s+] (US gay)
French-fried ice-cream [1950s+] (gay)
gnat butter [1900s-40s] (US)
gravy [mid-18C+]
honey [19C+]
hot fat [1990s]
hot milk [19C]
jam [1960s+] (US Black)
jelly [17C-19C]
joy juice [1980s+] (US)
juice [early 18C+]
living sauce [1990s]
love custard [1990s]
love juice [late 19C+]
man's milk [1990s]

manfat [1990s]
melted butter [19C]
milk [mid-17C+]
nut [1990s] (US)
oyster [late 17C+]
pudding [late 17C+]
roe [mid-19C-1900s]
soul sauce [1980s+] (US gay)
Spanish rice [1960s]
sugar [1920s+] (US Black)
water of life [1950s+] (US Black)
whipped cream [1970s+] (US Black)

SMEGMA

cheese [mid-19C+] (US)
cock cheese [mid-19C+]
corn on the cob [1990s]
dick dolcelatte [1980s]
duck butter [1930s+] (US)
fumunda cheese [1980s+] (US campus)
gnat butter [1900s-40s] (US)
headcheese [20C]
helmet halva [1980s]
knob cheese [mid-19C+]
monterey jack [1990s] (US)
nob stilton [1990s]
pecker cheese [1990s]
willy wensleydale [1980s]

Girls

THE VAGINA

MONOSYLLABIC

cock [20C] (US South/US Black)
cono [1940s+] (US)
cony [early 17C+] (lit. 'rabbit')
cooch [20C] (US)
coot [1980s+] (US campus)
cooter [1980s+] (US campus)
cooze [1920s+] (US)
coynte [19C]
cunnikin [18C]
cunny [early 18C+]
cunt [mid-15C+]
cuntkin [18C]
cuntlet [18C]
cush [1950s-60s] (Arabic 'vagina')
cuzzy [20C] (US; lit. 'cousin')
ginch [1950s+] (dial. 'a small piece')
joint [1970s] (US)
monosyllable [18C-19C]
nookie [1960s+] (orig. US)
poon [1920s+] (US)
poonce/punce [late 19C+] (Yiddish *punse*)
poontang [1920s+] (orig. US; from French *putain*, 'whore')
pootenanny [1990s] (US Black)
pum-pum [1980s+] (W.I.; Krio *pumbe*, 'vulva')
pundu [1970s+] (S.Afr.)
punse [late 19C+] (Yiddish)
quaint [16C-late 19C]

THE PUDENDUM

ace of spades [20C] (US Black)
badger [1990s] (orig. US)
black ace [mid-17C]
bonnet [1990s]
chin rest [1990s] (i.e. during cunnilingus)
dickey-dido [20C]
downstairs [20C]
hairy wheel [mid-19C+] (Aus.)
half-moon [17C]
ha'penny [20C]
Herbie's bonnet/Herbie's beetle's bonnet [20C]
(refers esp. to a shaved pudendum; from its similarity
to the curving bonnet of the Volkswagen Beetle)
mo [late 19C+] (Aus./N.Z.; abbr. 'moustache')
velcro love triangle [1990s]

65

quem [early 18C+]
queynte [16C]
quiff [20C]
quim [early 18C+] (Welsh *cwm*, 'valley')
quimsby [early 18C+]
trim [20C] (US)
tun-tun [1950s+] (W.I./USVI)
tunti [1950s+] (W.I. Rasta)
twam/twammy/twim [20C]
vag [20C]
venerable monosyllable [18C-19C]

THE VAGINA IN RHYMING SLANG

rhyming with *cunt*
Berkeley hunt [1930s+]
Berkshire hunt [1930s+]
Birchington hunt [1930s+]
Burlington hunt [1930s+]
gasp and grunt [1930s+]
groan and grunt [1930s+]
growl and grunt [1930s+]
grumble and grunt [1930s+]
sharp and blunt [20C]
Sir Berkeley [1930s]
rhyming with *collar*
must-I-holler [1980s+] (US Black)
rhyming with *gash*
Leslie [1990s]
rhyming with *fanny*
Jack an' Danny [1990s]
rhyming with *twat*
dillypot [1930s-60s] (Aus.)

EQUATED WITH THE BUTTOCKS

arse [19C+]
blate [1990s]
blurt [1990s]
blut [1990s]
bumshop [mid-19C-1900s]

chuff [1940s+] (Aus./northern UK)
chuftie [1990s]
fan [19C]
fanny [mid-19C+]
fanny-artful [19C]
fanny-fair [19C]
gazookus [1970s] (US)
gee [1990s]
gee-gee [1950s+] (US)
grommet [late 19C-1940s] (US)
kazoo [1960s+]
minge [20C]
naf [mid-19C]
nether end [19C]
nether eye [19C]
nether lips [19C]
prat [19C+]
twange [1990s]

EUPHEMISTIC

affair [mid-19C]
agility [19C]
catherine wheel [20C]
cloth [19C]
commodity [19C]
confessional [19C]
cornucopia [19C]
crown of sense [late 17C]
dearest bodily part [late 16C-early 17C]
down below [20C]

front bottom

67

down there [20C]
downstairs [19C]
downy bit [late 19C]
etcetera [late 16C-early 17C]
factotum [late 19C] (lit. 'man of all work')
fancy-bit [19C]
feminine gender [late 19C]
fie for shame [19C]
flange [1990s] (orig. US)
fleshly part [19C]
fornicator [19C]
funniment [19C]
funny bit [19C]
gallimaufry [19C] (lit. 'a mess of food')

gizmo/gismo [1940s+]
hey-nonny-no [late 16C-mid-18C]
it [19C]
jewel [19C]
knick-knack [19C]
little pal [19C]
little sister [19C]
love-flesh [19C]
main vein [1950s+]
masterpiece [18C]
modicum [late 17C-mid-19C]
mute [1970s]
name it not [19C]
nameless [19C]
naughty [mid-19C-1900s]
never-out [19C]
nonesuch/nonsuch [18C-19C]

nonny-no [16C]
novelty [18C]
number nip [19C]
old ding [19C]
old lady [mid-19C+]
old thing [mid-19C+]
ornament [19C]
package [1980s+] (US)
poor man's blessing [19C]
quid [19C] (Latin 'what')
quiver [19C]
quoniam [late 14C-early 18C] (Latin 'whereas')
rest and be thankful [19C]
sex [1930s+]
she [late 19C+]
t'aint/taint/taintmeat [1990s] (US)
that [19C+]
that there [20C]
that thing [1900s-40s] (US Black)
the ineffable [19C]
the place [20C]
the thing [20C]
thingamy [20C]
thingumabob [20C]
thingumajig [20C]
tu quoque [late 18C-early 19C] (Latin 'you too')
undeniable [19C]
upright grin [mid-19C]
vertical smile [20C]
what-do-you-call-it [19C]
where the monkey sleeps [20C]

where Uncle's doodle goes [mid-late 19C]
worst part [16C]
you-know-what [20C]
you-know-where [20C]

LITERARY

ABC [19C] (i.e. 'the beginning')
agreeable ruts of life [18C]
aphrodisiacal tennis court [17C]
bath of birth [19C]
belle-chose [14C] (French 'beautiful thing')
best in Christendom [late 17C]
book-binder's wife [late 19C] (she 'manufactures in sheets')
bull's eye [late 17C]
circle [19C]
copyhold [17C]
Cyprian arbour [early 17C] (*Cyprian* = whore)
Cyprian cave [early 17C]
Cyprian strait [early 17C]
eye that weeps most when best pleased [19C]
gear [late 19C+]
gymnasium [17C]
Hans Carvel's Ring [late 18C]
hypogastrian cranny [mid-17C] (Greek *hypograstrium*,
    that part of the body below the belly and above
    the privates)
justum [mid-17C] (Latin 'a suitable thing')
lamp of love [19C]
leading article [mid-19C-1900s]
leather [mid-16C+]

life's dainty [19C]
love's harbour [19C]
love's paradise [19C]
mine of pleasure [mid-19C]
Mount-Faulcon [late 16C]
mouth that cannot bite [late 17C-early 18C]
mouth that says no words [18C]
nest in the bush [late 17C]
part of India [late 16C-early 17C] (from the shape of
    the pudendum)
skincoat [16C]
target [late 17C]
the mouth thankless [early-mid-19C]
tirly-whirly [late 18C] (Scot. 'winding' or 'intricate')
wame [late 18C] (Scot. *wame* = womb)
weather gig [late 17C-early 18C]

71

MYTH AND LEGEND

abraham's bosom [19C]
adam's own altar [19C]
almanack [late 19C-1900s]
alpha and omega [19C]
altar of hymen [19C]
altar of love [19C]
altar of pleasure [19C]
amulet [19C]
boskage of Venus [19C]
Cupid's Alley [mid-19C]
Cupid's anvil [19C]
Cupid's arbour [19C]

Cupid's cave [19C]
Cupid's cloister [19C]
Cupid's corner [19C]
Cupid's cupboard [19C]
hogstye of Venus [19C]
mother of all masons [19C]
mother of all saints [late 18C-early 19C]
mother of all souls [late 18C]
mother of St Patrick [18C]
mother of St Paul [early 19C]
Venus's highway [19C]
Venus's honeypot [19C]
Venus's mark [19C]
Venus's secret cell [19C]

72

A PLACE FOR THE PENIS

bag [late 19C-1930s]
bag of tricks [19C]
bird's nest [20C]
Bluebeard's closet [19C]
box [1940s+]
bucket [1990s] (a large or loose vagina)
caldron [19C]
canister [20C]
cellar [19C]
cellar-door [19C]
cellarage [19C]
chuff-box [20C]
cock-chafer [late 19C]
cock hall [late 18C-1900s]

ITCHING JENNY AND OTHER IMPROPER NAMES

Aunt Maria [1900s] (*Aunt Maria* = 'fire' in rhy. sl.; the vagina gets 'hot')

Boris [1990s] (from the song 'Boris the Spider')

Buckinger's boot [late 18C] (worn on the 'third leg')

Davy Crockett's hat [1990s]

itching Jenny [19C]

Jacob's ladder [19C] (the penis 'climbs up it')

jack nasty face [mid-19C]

Lady Berkeley [19C] (rhy. sl. from *Berkshire Hunt*)

Lady Jane [mid-19C+]

Maddikin [late 18C-mid-19C]

Madge [late 18C-19C]

Madge Howlett [late 18C-19C] (lit. 'a barn-owl')

Mary Jane [mid-19C-1930s]

McMuff [1990s]

Michael [1930s] (Aus.; rhy. sl. *Michael Hunt*)

Mick [1930s+] (Aus.)

Mickey [1960s+] (Aus.)

Mickey Mouse [1930s-40s] (US)

Miss Brown [late 18C]

Miss Laycock [late 18C-early 19C]

Molly's Hole [19C]

spinning Jenny [19C]

tickle Thomas [19C]

Virginia [1990s] (US)

73

NOW YOU SHOW ME YOURS

cock-holder [19C]
cock-locker [1980s]
cock-loft [19C]
cock pit [late 18C-20C]
cockshire [late 18C-20C]
cockshy [19C]
cogie [19C] (Scot. 'milk pail')
confessional [19C]
corner-cupboard [19C]
cradle [19C]
cuckoo's nest [19C]
doodle-case [late 19C] (*doodle* = penis)
doodle-sack [19C]
evening socket [1990s] (the man 'plugs in' at night)
fuzzy cup [1970s+] (US Black)
goldfinch's nest [19C]
home sweet home [late 19C-1920s]
jigger [mid-19C]
joy box [1970s] (US)
kennel [late 17C-19C]
kettle [17C]
keyhole [late 19C-1920s]
lock [19C]
lock of locks [18C]
locker [19C]
love glove [1980s+] (US)
lucky bag [19C]
machine [late 19C]
miraculous pitcher [late 18C-mid-19C]
naggie [19C-1900s]
needlecase [19C]

nest [late 18C; 1920s+]
niche-cock [late 18C-late 19C]
parking lot [1960s-70s] (US)
pen [mid-19C-1900s]
penwiper [19C]
phoenix nest [19C] (it makes the penis 'rise again')
pin-case [19C]
pin-cushion [19C]
pink velvet sausage wallet [1990s]
pintlecase [19C] (*pintle* = penis)
pipkin [17C]
pitcher [late 17C-1900s]
pitcher that holds water with the mouth down
    [late 17C-1900s]
plumber's toolbag [1990s]
pole hole [1970s+]
pouch [1940s-50s]
prick-purse [19C]
prickholder [19C]
quarry [18C]
rag box [1970s+] (US Black)
sack [late 17C]
scabbard [19C]
serpent socket [1990s]
sheath [19C]
shot-locker [20C] (US)
sleeve [1990s] (US campus)
spleuchan [late 18C] (Scot. 'a tobacco pouch')
standing room for one [19C]
toolbox [19C+]
tool chest [19C]

A RECEPTACLE FOR SEMEN

beehive [19C]
brat-getting place [19C]
butter-boat [19C]
certificate of birth [19C]
churn [19C]
cream jug [19C]
glamity [1980s+] (W.I./UK Black teen; dial. 'wet and sticky')
gluepot [20C]
hive [mid-late 19C]
honeypot [early 18C+]
lather-maker [19C]
melting pot [19C]
milk pan [late 18C-1900s]
milking pail [late 19C]
milt market [19C] (*milt* = the roe of the male fish)
milt shop [19C]
seminary [19C]
spunk-pot [1990s]
stadge [1990s] (from 'stodge', i.e. thick and sticky;
    refers esp. to the vagina of a fat woman)

EQUATED WITH THE PUBIC HAIR

ace [mid-late 19C]
ace of spades [20C] (US Black)
bear-trapper's hat [1960s+]
bearded lady [1960s+]
black bess [19C]
black jock [19C]

sporran

broom [19C]
bun [17C]
dingleberry [1970s]
fluff [1970s+]
frizzle [20C]
fur [18C+]
furry bicycle stand
    [1990s]
hairy cup [1990s]
hairy doughnut [20C]
hairy goblet [1990s]
hairy lasoo [1990s]
Hairyfordshire [mid-19C]
mohair knickers [1990s] (an extremely hairy vagina)
moosey [1920s-50s] (US; dial. 'soft', 'over-ripe')
muff [late 17C+]
old frizzle [18C-late 19C]
oracle [late 18C-late 19C]
patch [19C]
red ace/red c. [mid-late 19C]
rufus [19C]
sporran [19C]

FEAR AND LOATHING DOWN UNDER

bit of rough [mid-19C+]
bite [16C-18C; 20C]
blind eye [late 18C-1900s]
bumbo [late 18C+] (lit. 'alligator')
carnal-trap [16C]
catch-em-alive-o [mid-19C]
claptrap [20C]
clout [1990s]
crush [late 19C+]
dumb glutton [late 18C]
dumb oracle [18C]
dumb squint [18C]
eel pot [late 18C-early 19C]
eel-skinner [late 18C-early 19C]
fire [19C]
firelock [19C]
fireplace [19C]
fires of hell [19C]
firework [19C]
fly-catcher [19C]
flycage [19C]
flytrap [19C]
fool trap [late 16C-early 18C]
forge [19C]
fort [19C]
fortress [19C]
grindstone [mid-19C+]
growler [1990s]
gyve/gyvel [late 18C] (lit. 'a shackle')

hone [17C] (lit. 'grinder')
man-trap [late 18C-early 19C]
mangle [19C]
manhole [20C]
mark of the beast [18C]
mill [late 18C-early 19C]
mousetrap [late 19C+]
nasty [mid-19C]
parts of shame [19C]
prannie/pranny [late 19C+] (Scot. *pran* = to crush)
prick-scourer [19C]
prick-skinner [19C]
rasp [late 19C-1900s]
rattle bollocks [18C]
rattlesnake canyon [20C]
rob the ruffian [19C]
rough-and-ready [mid-19C]
rough-and-tumble [mid-19C]
rough-o [19C]
skin-the-pizzle [mid-19C-1900s]
snapper [1960s+] (US)
snapping turtle [20C]
snatch [late 19C+]
snatch box [late 19C]
snatch-blatch [late 19C-1910s]
sperm-sucker [19C]
staff breaker [19C]
staff climber [19C]
stank [1970s+] (US Black)
stench trench [20C]
stink [1970s+] (US Black)

stinkpot [1950s-70s] (US Black)
suck and swallow [19C]
touch 'em up [19C]
tuzzymuzzy [early 18C-19C] (lit. 'dishevelled')
vacuum [19C]
wastepipe [19C]
whetting corn/stone [17C] (lit. 'a grindstone')

THE HOLE

black hole [19C]
black ring [19C]
bob and hit [19C] (rhy. sl. 'pit')
bore [18C]

bottomless pit [late 18C-early 19C]
bung [1960s] (US)
bunghole [1960s+] (US)
button-hole [19C]
cave of harmony [mid-19C]
dark [19C]
dark-hole [19C]
drain [19C]
fuckhole [late 19C+]
fun hatch [1990s]
furry hoop [20C]
gape over the garter [mid-19C]
glory hole [1920s+] (orig. US)
golden doughnut [20C]
grummet [19C] (lit. 'a washer')
gully [19C]
gully hole [19C]

hole [late 16C+]
hole of content [19C]
hole of holes [19C]
Holloway [mid-19C-1920s] (puns on 'hollow way')
hoop [1930s+] (US prison)
horse-collar [19C]
inkwell [1970s] (US)
joy hole [1930s-40s] (US Black)
love hole [1980s+] (US)
lower mouth [mid-19C]
maw [mid-19C+]
mousehole [19C]
Olympic pool [20C]
open charms [19C]
passion pit [19C]
pigeonhole [late 16C-late 17C] (UK Und.)
pit [early 19C+]
pit hole [19C]
pit mouth [19C]
pit of darkness [19C]
poke-hole [late 19C+]
pokey [20C] (orig. W.I. teen)
poking-hole [late 19C+]
porthole [17C]
queen of holes [19C]
ring [16C-18C]
second hole from the back of the neck [20C]
socket [late 17C-18C]
sportsman's gap [19C]
sportsman's hole [19C]
upper Holloway [19C]

THE SLIT

alcove [19C]
arbour [19C]
axe wound [1990s]
breach [19C]
canyon [1970s+]
chasm [19C]
chink [18C]
cleft [19C]
cleft of flesh [19C]
cloven spot [mid-18C]
crack [16C+]
cranny [19C]
crevice [19C]
crinkum-crankum [late 18C-early 19C]
Cupid's furrow [19C]
dimple [19C]
everlasting wound [mid-19C]
furrow [19C]
gap [18C+]
gape [mid-19C]
gaper [19C]
gash [18C+]
the great divide [mid-19C]
groove [1920s-60s] (US Black)
grotto [19C]
gulf [19C]
gusset [17C]
inglenook [19C]
nick [18C-late 19C]

nick in the notch [19C]
nick-nack [mid-19C]
nock [late 16C]
notch [18C-mid-19C]
one-ended furrow [19C]
placket/placket box [17C] (lit. 'the slit at the top of
    a petticoat')
slash [20C] (US)
slice [20C]
slice of life [20C]
slit [mid-17C+]
slot [1940s+] (Aus./N.Z.)
snicket [1990s] (lit. 'a narrow passage')
spasm chasm [1990s]
split [1910s+] (Aus./US)
trench [19C]
twat [mid-17C+] (dial. *twitchel*, 'a narrow passage')

OBJECTS AND PERSONIFICATIONS

beauty [19C]
bed fellow [19C]
booty [1920s+] (US Black; lit. 'body')
brown madam [late 18C]
case [17C]
chum [late 19C]
coupler [18C]
fiddle [19C]
flap [17C]
fly by night [19C]
forewoman [mid-19C]

futz [1940s+] (lit. 'a trifle')
gigg [18C] (lit. 'a light carriage')
goatmilker [mid-19C]
hat [mid-18C-mid-19C]
housewife [19C]
instrument [19C]
itcher [late 17C-early 18C]
jing-jang [19C]
jock [late 18C+]
joxy [20C]
kaifa/keifer/kyfer [late 19C+]
    (Arabic *kayf* = absolute enjoyment)
lap [late 16C]
lips [1990s] (US Black)
little sister [19C]
long-eye [mid-late 19C]
lute [19C] (an instrument to be 'played')
milliner's shop [19C]
old hat [late 17C-late 19C]
old woman [late 18C+]
omnibus [mid-late 19C] (it is 'ridden' by all)
pink-eye [20C] (US)
pouter [19C]
saddle [late 17C-early 19C]
sampler [19C] (something one 'sews')
shakebag [early 18C-late 19C]
undertaker [19C]
vade-mecum [19C] (lit. 'come with me')
wanton ace [19C]
winker [1970s] (it 'winks' like a 'vertical eye')

THE MONEY-MAKER

bank [19C]
bargain bucket [1990s]
bazaar [19C]
boodle [1980s] (US)
breadwinner [19C]
budget [19C]
commodity [19C]
custom house [late 18C]
Eve's custom house [late 18C]
exchequer [early-mid-16C]
ha'penny [20C]
money [late 18C+]

FORTUNES AND PORTIONS

Irish fortune [19C] (the vagina)
Rochester portion [late 17C-early 19C] ('two torn
    smocks and what nature gave')
Tetbury portion [18C] ('a cunt and a clap'; i.e. sexual
    intercourse followed by a dose of venereal disease)
Tipperary fortune [late 18C-early 19C] ('Two *town
    lands* [the breasts], *stream's town* [the pudend] and
    ballinocack [the anus]')
Whitechapel fortune [late 17C-18C] ('a clean gown
    and a pair of pattens')
Whitechapel portion [late 17C-18C]

moneybox [19C]
money machine [1960s-70s] (US)
money-maker [late 19C+]
money-spinner [19C]
nature's treasury [19C]
ninepence [late 19C+]
purse [late 17C-18C]
receipt of custom [late 18C]
till [19C]
toll dish [17C]
treasure [19C]
treasure of love [mid-late 18C]
treasure of pleasure [mid-late 18C]
trot [18C-late 19C] (lit. 'a prostitute')
ware [late 18C-early 19C] (i.e. 'goods')

TOPOGRAPHICAL

Antipodes [mid-19C-1920s] (i.e. 'down under')
attic [1900s]
blind alley [late 19C]
Botany Bay [19C] (i.e. 'down under')
Cape Horn [19C]
Cape Of Good Hope [19C]
Cock Inn [19C-20C]
Cock Lane [19C]
County Down [19C]
cunny-burrow [17C]
cunny warren [18C]
Cupid's arms [19C]
Cupid's hotel [19C]

custom house goods [late 18C] ('the stock in trade of
a prostitute, because fairly entered')
ditch [19C]
Downshire [19C]
Exeter Hall [19C] (a teasing reference to a place best
known for temperance meetings)
generating place [19C]
geography [1920s-30s]
happy hunting grounds [19C] (orig. US)
heaven [18C]
hell [18C]
hotel [19C]
house under the hill [19C]
Jack Straw's Castle [19C]
Lapland [mid-late 19C]
Leather-Lane [19C]
leaving shop [mid-late 19C]
lob's pound [late 16C-early 19C] (*lob* = penis)
locker [19C]
lodgings [19C]
love nest [1990s] (US)
low countries [18C]
lowlands [late 18C-mid-19C]
Mons Meg [19C] (from the gaping mouth of the cannon
kept at Edinburgh Castle)
mossy cottage [1990s]
Mount Pleasant [mid-19C]
Netherlands [18C] (the 'low country')
nursery [19C]
palace of pleasure [19C]
parlour [19C]

pleasure ground [19C]
pleasure place [19C]
premises [19C]
privy paradise [19C]
pulpit [19C]
Shooter's Hill [19C]
South Pole [19C]
thatched house under the hill [19C]
third base [1940s+] (US; thus
    a 'home run' = intercourse)
under-belongings [19C]
undercarriage [1990s]
under-dimple [19C]
underworld [19C]
vestry [19C]

CENTRALITY

axis [19C]
central cut [19C]
central office [19C]
central furrow [19C]
centre of attraction [19C]
centre of bliss [late 18C]
centrique part [17C]
middle cut [1970s] (US Black)
middle kingdom [19C]
midlands [19C]

ROAD TO
HEAVEN
CLOSED

THE ROAD OR TUNNEL

alley [19C]
baby chute [1990s]
Cock Alley [18C+]
covered way [19C]
crooked way [19C]
Dead End Street [19C]
flue [late 19C+] (US)
highway [20C]
joy trail [1970s+]
love canal [1980s+] (US)
love-lane [mid-19C]
main avenue [19C]
much-travelled highway [19C]
pipe [1960s+]
red lane [20C]
road [late 16C-early 17C]
road to a christening [19C]
road to heaven [19C]
smock alley [18C]
spew alley [19C]
tunnel [19C]
turnpike [19C]
twatchel [mid-17C-early 19C] (lit. 'a passage')
velvet tunnel [1990s]

THE ENTRANCE

belly entrance [19C]
entrance [19C]
forecastle [19C]
fore-court [19C]
foregut [19C]
fore-hatch [19C]
fore-room [19C]
front attic [19C]
front bottom [1990s]
front bum [1990s]
front door [19C+] (US Black)
front entrance [19C]
front garden/gate [19C]
front gut [19C]
front parlour [19C]
front room [early 19C]
front window [19C]
Gate of Horn [19C]
gate of life [late 18C]
gut entrance [19C]
hatchway [mid-late 19C]
ivory gate [19C]
Marble Arch [mid-19C]
under-entrance [19C]
way-in [19C]
wicket [19C] (i.e. a 'gate')

HORTICULTURAL

beauty spot [19C]
belly dale [19C]
belly dingle [19C]
bower of bliss [17C-19C]
evergreens [19C]
flower of chivalry [19C]
flowerpot [19C]
fruitful vine [19C]
garden [19C]
garden of Eden [16C-17C; 20C]
garden of pleasure [19C]
gentleman's pleasure-garden [late 19C-1900s]
green meadow [mid-19C]
hortus [18C] (Latin 'garden')
lady flower [mid-19C] (US)
living fountain [mid-17C]
miraculous cairn [19C]
moss rose [19C]
mossy bank [19C]
mossy cell [19C]
mossy face [19C]
nature [19C] (US Black)
nature's tufted treasure [19C]
nettle bed [early 18C-mid-19C]
orchard [19C]
parsley bed [early 18C-mid-19C]
rose [18C+]
seed plot [19C]
shady spring [mid-19C]

AQUATIC

barge [1950s+] (US)
boat [1950s] (US Black)
bore [18C]
damp [1950s+]
ditch [19C]
drain [19C]
duckpond [19C]
dyke [19C]
fountain of love [19C]
gutter [19C]
harbour [19C]
harbour of hope [19C]
peculiar river [late 16C]
pisser [20C]
pleasure boat [19C]
puddle [late 19C-1910s]
pump dale [17C]
rigol [17C-18C] (lit. 'watercourse')
slithery [1930s+]
sluice [17C]
stream's town [late 18C-early 19C]
water-course [19C]
water-gap [19C]
water-mill [early 19C]
waterbox [19C]
wayside ditch [19C]
wayside fountain [19C]

FISHY

bearded clam [1960s+]
bearded oyster [1910s+]
bit of fish [mid-19C-1900s]
bit of skate [late 19C+]
clam [20C] (US)
clambake [1990s] (US)
cod trench [1990s]
fish [mid-19C+]
fish market [mid-19C-1900s]
fish mitten [1990s]
fish-tank [1980s+]
free fishery [late 19C-1900s]
fuzzy lap flounder [1990s]
haddock pastie [1990s]
hirsute oyster [1990s]
kipper [1950s]
kipper box [1990s]
lobster pot [19C]
oyster [late 17C+]
oyster-catcher [late 19C]
periwinkle [mid-19C-1900s]
red snapper [20C] (US)
scat [1970s+] (US Black)
scate [17C] (i.e. 'skate')
split kipper [1990s]
tench [mid-19C]
trout [1950s-60s] (US Black)
tuna [1950s+] (orig. US Black)
whelk [mid-late 19C]

CULINARY

bit on a fork [mid-19C]
bread [1950s-60s] (orig. US Black)
butter [1980s+] (US Black)
cut and come again [19C]
holy Dorito [1990s]
kitchen [mid-19C]
milk jug [late 18C-1900s]
milker [late 19C-1900s]
mossy doughnut [1940s] (US)
mustard pot [late 19C+]
oven [late 17C-1910s]
P.E.E.P. [1980s+] (US; '*p*erfectly *e*xcellent *e*ating *p*ussy')
roasting jack [19C]
saltcellar [19C]
salting [1950s+] (W.I./Rasta; lit. 'salty thing')
tit-bit [mid-17C-late 18C]

THE PATISSERIE

bit of jam [late 19C]
bonne-bouche [19C] (French 'a pleasant taste')
brownie [1970s]
cakes [1960s+] (US Black)
coffee-shop [19C]
doughnut [1980s]
fig [mid-19C]
finger pie [20C]
flitter [19C] (US; dial. 'a pancake')
fur pie [20C]

hair pie [1930s+] (orig. US)
honey altar [1990s]
jam [1980s+] (US Black)
jam cookie [1990s]
jampot [late 19C+]
jelly [1920s+] (US Black)
jelly bag [17C]
jelly box [1920s+] (orig. US)
jelly roll [1920s-40s] (orig. US)
lollipop [1960s+]
muffin [1950s+]
pancake [19C+]
pie [1950s+] (US)
sugar basin [19C]
sweet potato pie [1980s+] (US Black)
yum yum [late 19C+]

THE BUTCHER'S SHOP

bacon hole [20C]
bacon sandwich [20C]
bearded taco [1950s+] (US)
beef [late 18C+]
bit of meat [early 18C+]
bit of mutton [19C]
bit of pork [18C-1900s]
butcher's window [19C+]
butcher's shop [19C]
catsmeat [19C]
chopped liver [20C]
dripping pan [18C]

fart-daniel [19C] (lit. 'a sucking pig')
furburger [1960s+]
fuzzburger [1960s+]
G [1950s+] (US Black; abbr. 'goodies')
gammon [1990s]
gorilla burger [1990s]
gravy-giver [19C]
gravy-maker [19C]
gristle-gripper [1990s]
laced mutton [17C-mid-19C]
meat [late 16C+]
mutton [16C]
nanty crackling [late 19C-1920s]
prime cut [1970s+]

split mutton [17C-19C]

THE CABBAGE PATCH

apple [1970s+] (US Black)
cabbage [late 19C]
cabbage field [19C]
cabbage garden [19C]
cabbage patch [19C]
cauliflower [late 18C-19C]
cherry pie [late 19C+]
date [1910s+] (Aus./N.Z.)
greengrocery [mid-19C]
groceries [19C] (US gay)
lemon [1930s+] (US Black)
medlar [late 18C-early 19C]
mushroom [19C]

orange [late 17C]
pineapple [1910s]
plum tree [17C]
split apricot [late 17C-19C]
split fig [late 17C-early 19C]

THE MENAGERIE

beaver [1920s+] (US)
bird [1960s-70s] (US)
black cat with its throat cut [1950s+]
bug [1980s] (US)
bunny [18C+]
cat [1950s+]
catty-cat [1970s+] (US Black)
chat [18C] (French 'cat')
chinchilla [20C] (US)
civet [18C-19C]
coyote [19C] (US)
cushat [19C] ('a wood pigeon')
donkey's yawn [1990s]
dormouse [19C]
fluff [1970s+] (US Black)
fur [18C+]
kitty [20C]
kitty-cat [20C]
magpie's nest [20C] (US Black)
malkin [late 17C-18C] (Scot. *malkin* = cat)
mink [20C] (US)
mole-catcher [late 19C-1910s]
monkey [late 19C+] (Aus./US)

mouser [early 19C-1900s]
p [1990s] (US Black; abbr. 'pussy')
p-maker [mid-19C-1900s] (i.e. 'piss-maker')
pink [1950s] (W.I.)
poes [1960s+] (S.Afr.; i.e. 'pussy')
poozle [late 19C+] (i.e. 'pussy')
puss [17C+]
pussy [mid-19C+]
pussycat [19C+] (US Black)
rat [1990s]
rooster [mid-19C-1900s]
rough-malkin [late 17C-18C] (lit. 'rough cat')
spadger [1990s] (Aus.; dial. 'a sparrow')
squelchy monkey [1990s]
stoat [1990s]
tail [late 17C+]
tit [early 18C+]
titmouse [mid-17C-late 18C]

FEMALE PUBIC HAIR

area [19C]
banner [19C]
beard [early 18C; late 19C+]
bearskin [19C]
beaver [1920s+] (orig. US)
belly bristles [19C]
belly whiskers [late 19C]
bikini burger [1990s]

$E = mc^2$

black jock [late 18C]
broccoli [1980s+]
broom [19C]
brush [1930s+]
bun [17C]
busby [19C]
bush [1920s+]
Bushy Park [mid-19C]
carpet [1980s+] (US campus)
cat [mid-19C]
copper crack [1990s] (i.e. ginger pubic hair)
cotton [1970s+] (US Black)
cotton and wool [19C]
county down [19C]
crown and feathers [mid-late 19C]
cunnyskin [19C]
cunt-curtain [19C]
damber-bush [19C] (lit. 'dame bush')
Davy Crockett's hat [1990s]
dickweed [1990s] (US)
dickwheat [1990s] (US)
dilberry bush [mid-late 19C]
Downshire [19C]
Einstein [1980s+] (US campus; refers to the physicist's
    crinkly hair)
fancy work [20C]
feather [18C]
fern [1950s+] (US)
fleece [19C]
fluff [mid-19C]
forest [mid-19C+]

front-door mat [1930s-60s]

fur [18C+]

furbelow [18C-mid-19C]

furze-bush [mid-19C]

fuzz [1980s+]

fuzzies [1960s] (US)

garden [19C]

ginge minge [1990s] (i.e. ginger pubic hair)

gooseberry bush [19C]

gorilla salad [1960s+] (US gay)

grass [1910s]

green grove [19C]

grove of eglantine [19C]

hair court [19C]

hairy oracle [late 18C-mid-19C]

hairy ring [19C]

hebe [early-mid-18C] (*Hebe* was the goddess of youth)

hedge on the dyke [19C]

lady's low toupee [19C]

lawn [1950s+]

lemon [1930s+] (US Black)

lower wig [19C]

map of Tassie [1990s] (Aus.; from its supposed similarity to
    the shape of Tasmania)

moss [19C+]

moss rose [19C]

mossy bank [19C+]

mossy cell [19C+]

mossy face [late 18C-early 19C]

mott-carpet [19C]

mott-fleece [19C] (lit. 'woman fleece')

muff [late 17C+]
mustard-and-cress [19C]
nether beard [mid-19C]
nether eyebrow [19C]
nether eyelashes [19C]
nether whiskers [19C]
parsley [mid-19C]
plush [19C]
pubes [1950s+]
pubickers [1990s] (Irish)
pussy hair [1970s+]
quim bush [late 18C+]
quim whiskers [19C]
quim wig [19C]
rat [1990s]
red ace [mid-late 19C]
red c. [mid-late 19C] (lit. 'red cunt')
rusty bucket [1990s]
scrubbing brush [mid-19C+] (Aus.)
scut [late 16C+] (*scut* = rabbit's tail)
shaving brush [20C]
short and curlies [20C]
shrubbery [19C]
Sigourney Weaver [1990s] (rhy. sl. 'beaver')
silent beard [19C]
snatch-thatch [18C]
snuggy [1940s-50s] (US)
squirrel [1970s] (US campus)
stubble [18C-20C]
sweet briar [17C]
tail-feathers [late 17C+]

thatch [mid-19C]
toupee [mid-18C-mid-19C]
tuft [1970s+]
twat-rug [late 19C-1900s]
vines [1970s] (US Black)
whin-bush [19C]
whisker [1940s+] (Aus.)
wool [20C]

THE LABIA

breakfast of champions [1990s]
bum bacon [1990s]
cat's head cut open [19C]
chicken wings [1990s]
columns of Venus [18C]
cuntocks [1990s]
dew-flaps [1990s]
double-sucker [late 19C]
ear between the legs [19C]
fat cock [late 19C]
fish lips [1990s]
flaps [1960s+]
fuck flaps [1990s]
garden gate [mid-19C]
gate in the orchard [19C]
Hottentot apron [20C] (refers to elongated labia)
knicker bacon [1990s]
meat curtains [1990s]

passion flaps [1990s]
piss flaps/flappers [20C]
quim nuts [1990s] (US)
saddle bags [1990s]
split/spread/wide-open beaver [1970s+]
     (i.e. the wide-open vagina, as in hard-core pornography)
steak drapes [1990s]
sushi taco [1990s]
undermeat [1990s]
vertical bacon sandwich [1990s] (US)

THE CLITORIS

baby in the boat [1930s]
bald man in a boat [20C]
bean [1990s]
boy in the boat [late 19C+]
budd [1990s]
button [19C+]
dick [1960s] (US)
dingleberry [1970s]
dot [1970s+] (lesbian)
fanny flange [1990s]
joy button/buzzer [1970s+] (US)
little boy in the boat [20C]
little man [20C]
little old man in the boat [late 19C-1900s; 20C]
little ploughman [19C]
little shame tongue [19C]
love button [1990s] (US)
man in the boat [late 19C+]

nuts [20C] (US Black)
spare tongue [1960s]
taste bud [1960s+]

THE HYMEN

bean [1940s] (US)
cherry [1930s+] (orig. US)
clam [20C] (US)
maid's ring [late 19C]
nature's privy seal [19C]

VAGINAL SECRETIONS

bitch butter [1970s] (US Black)
clamjam [1990s]
come [1940s+]
cream [late 19C+]
crotch oil [1980s+] (US)
drippings [18C]
fanny batter [1990s]
flap snot [1990s]
French dip [1950s+] (refers to precoital fluid)
goose-grease [late 19C]
gravy [mid-18C+]
love juice [late 19C+]

THE BREASTS

baby bumpers [1960s+]
bags [1930s+] (US)
balangas [1980s+] (US)
balcony [1940s+] (Aus.)
balls [1950s-60s] (US)
bazongas [1970s+]
bazoom [1950s+]
bazoombas [1980s+] (US)
beautiful pair of brown eyes [1940s-60s]
berkeleys [late 19C] (Romani *berk*, breast)
bibble chunks [1990s]
blubber [late 18C+]
blubber bags [late 18C-20C]
bongos [1980s+] (US)
boob [1940s+] (orig. US)
boobies [1930s+] (orig. US)
bouncers [1950s-70s]
B.S.H.'s [1960s-70s] (*British Standard Handfuls*)
bubbies [17C]
bubby [20C] (W.I.)
buffers [late 19C+]
bumpers [1970s+]
chabbies/chabs [1990s] (i.e. 'chubbies')
chabobs [1960s] (US)
chalubbies [1970s] (US)
charlies [mid-19C+]
Charlie Wheelers [1940s+] (Aus.; from *Charles Wheeler*,
    a painter of nudes)
charms [mid-19C+]

chebs [1990s]
chest flesh [1990s]
chichibangas [1960s+] (US)
choozies [1990s] (Aus.)
credentials [1960s+] (US)
dangleberries [1970s+]
diddies/diddys [late 18C+]
dingleberries [1970s+]
ditties [1990s]
dollies [1960s+] (Irish)
dubbies [1960s+]
duds [1960s] (N.Z.)
filthy pillows [1990s]
fleshy bagpipes [1990s]
flight deck [1980s]
flip-flops [1920s+] (Aus.)
forebuttocks [early 18C]
gangsters [1990s] (orig. US)
glands [1970s+] (US)
globes [19C+]
globes of joy [1990s]
handles [1980s+] (US)
hands [1980s+] (US campus)
hand-warmers [1920s+] (Aus.)
hangers [1930s+] (Aus./US)
headlamps [1990s]
headlights [20C]
hooters [1970s+] (US)
jibs [1980s+] (US)
johnsons [1970s] (US)
knobs [1930s+]

knobbies [1930s+]

knockers [1930s+] (orig. US)

lotties [late 19C-1910s; 1990s]
    (from the music-hall singer *Lottie* Collins)

lumps [1990s] (US)

lungs [1950s+] (orig. US)

lung shot [1950s+]

lung warts [1940s+] (US)

maracas [1940s+] (US)

Mary Poppins [1960s] (US)

nards [1990s] (US)

nature's founts [19C]

nay nays [1950s+]

nice pair of eyes [1960s+]

ninnies [20C] (orig. US)

nubbies [late 19C+] (Aus.)

nuggies [1970s+] (US)

nugs [1990s] (US)

pair [1940s+]

panters [late 19C-1900s]

poonts [late 19C] (play on 'font' or 'fountain')

puppies [1990s]

rude parts [1970s+]

set [1960s+] (Aus.)

shock-absorbers [1950s+]

smiddys [1990s] (i.e. 'titties')

swingers [1920s+] (Aus.)

tatas [1980s+] (US)

tits [17C+]

tooraloorals [late 19C]

top ballocks/bollocks [late 19C+]

nice pair of eyes

THE BREASTS IN RHYMING SLANG

rhyming with *tits* and *titties*

brace and bits [20C] (US)

Bradford cities [1990s]

Brad Pitts/bradleys [1990s]

Bristol bits [1960s]

Bristols [1960s+]

cats and kitties [mid-20C]

fainting fits [1940s+]

fruppencies [1970s] (i.e. 'thruppences')

Jerseys [1960s+] (i.e. 'Jersey Cities')

Lewis and Witties [1940s-50s] (Aus.)

Manchester Cities/manchesters [20C] (Aus.)

racks/racks of meat [20C]

tale of two cities [1950s]

thousand pities [late 19C-1900s]

threepenny bits [late 19C+]

thrups [late 19C+] (i.e. 'thruppeny bits')

towns and cities [1900s-40s]

trey-bits [1950s+] (Aus./N.Z.)

rhyming with *breasts*

cabman's rests [late 19C+]

rhyming with *knockers*

mods and rockers [1960s]

rhyming with *melons*

Mary Ellens [20C]

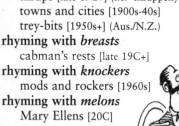

A TALE OF TWO CITIES

top buttocks [late 19C+]
top set [1980s]
top 'uns [1940s-50s]
upper deck [1940s] (Aus.)
waps/wap-waps [1990s] (lit. 'shakers')
willets [1990s]

LACTATIONAL

Bordens [1940s-70s] (US; from Borden's dairy)
cans [1950s-60s] (US)
chugs [1960s-70s] (US)
cream jugs [20C] (i.e. 'jugs')
dairy arrangements [1910s-20s]
dairy/dairies [late 18C; 1970s+]
dugs [19C]
elders [1960s+] (Irish; i.e. udders)
feeding bottles [20C]
fuck udders [1990s]
jugs [1950s] (orig. US)
mammaries [1970s+]
mams [1970s+]
milk bar [1950s+]
milk bottles [1930s+] (orig. Aus.)
milkers [20C]
milk factories [1940s-70s] (US)
milk jugs [1950s] (orig. US)
milk shakes [1910s-70s] (US)
milk shop/milk walk [19C]

109

milky way/way to bliss [18C]
ninny jugs [1970s] (US)
norks [1950s+] (Aus.; from Norco Ltd, butter manufacturer of NSW)
norgs [1950s+] (Aus.)
norgies [1950s+] (Aus.)
norkers [1950s+] (Aus.)
num-nums [1980s+] (US)
nungers [1960s] (Aus.)
udders [1930s+]

EDIBLE

apple-dumpling shop [late 18C]
apples [16C+]
avocados [1930s] (US)
baby's public house [late 19C]
baps [1990s] (orig. Ulster)
briskets [20C]
cakes [1970s+] (orig. US)
chestnuts [1950s-60s]
dinners/dinner buckets [20C] (US)
dumplings [early 18C+]
garbonzas [1980s+] (US)
goodies [1950s+] (US)
grapefruit [20C]
grapes [20C]
hogans [1960s+] (US; *hog* = eat greedily)
jujubes [1970s+]
lemons [1940s+] (US)
lollies [20C]

lunchcounter [1960s] (US)
lunchpail [1960s] (US)
mangoes [1980s+] (US)
meat market [late 19C+]

MILITARY

artillery [1920s+] (US)
bazookas [1960s+]
bombers [1970s] (US)
bombs [1960s-70s] (US)
breastworks [early 19C+]
Cupid's kettledrums [late 18C-early 19C]
equipment [1940s+]
field artillery [1920s+] (US)
guns [1950s+] (US Black)
rockets [1990s]
T.N.T. [1960s+] (i.e. 'two nifty tits')

LARGE BREASTS

balloons [1940s+]
blamps [1990s] (i.e. 'big headlamps')
bodacious tatas [1980s+] (US campus)
bubby [20C] (W.I.)
bushel bubby [late 18C] (a woman with large breasts)
cantilever bust [1950s+] (Aus.)
coconuts [late 19C-1900s]
funbags [1960s+]
funsacks [1960s+]
gazongas [20C]

111

gazonkas [1990s]

gazungas [20C]

gib teesurbs [mid-19C+] ('big breasts' in backslang)

honkers [1970s+] (US)

Irish evidence [1960s] (gay)

kahoonas [1990s]

lollos [1950s] (Aus.)

melons [1950s+]

mildreds [1990s] (large breasts on an older woman)

Miss/Mrs Van-Neck [late 18C-early 19C] (a woman with large breasts)

mountains [1970s+] (US Black)

party tits [1990s] (i.e. surgically enlarged breasts)

plumpies [1990s]

prize faggots [late 19C] (lit. 'larger than average faggots')

rack [1960s+] (US)

rib cushions [1990s]

shoulder boulders [1990s]

structural engineering [1950s+] (Aus.)

t.b. [1920s+] (Aus.; i.e. 'two beauts')

threateners [1990s]

tremblers [1960s+]

two puppies fighting in a bag [1970s+] (i.e. very large, poorly contained breasts)

wallopies [1970s+] (US campus)

watermelons [1980s+] (US campus)

whamdanglers [1990s]

SMALL BREASTS

bee-stings [1950s+] (orig. US)
berries [1970s+] (US Black)
boobus [1990s] (US Black)
chapel hat pegs [20C]
cherries [20C] (US)
eyes [1950s+]
fried eggs [1930s+]
kittens' noses [1990s]
mosquito bites [1970s+] (US campus)
two raisins on a bread board [20C]

THE NIPPLES

berries [1970s+] (US Black)
button [1960s] (US)
chapel hat pegs [20C]
cherries [20C] (US)
eyes [1950s+]
jalobies [1960s+]
kittens' noses [1990s]
nips [1970s+] (US)
raspberries [1970s+]
tits [17C+]

Bottoms

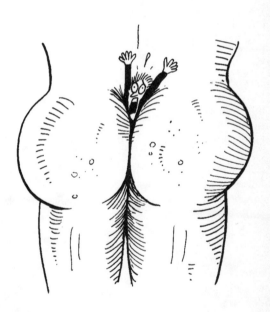

THE ANUS AND RECTUM

ars musica [late 18C-19C] (Latin 'the musical art')
back door [mid-18C+]
back-door trumpet [mid-19C+]
back eye [1950s+]
backslice [mid-19C]
backslit [mid-19C]
barking spider [1980s+]
blind eye [late 18C-1900s]
blot [1940s+] (Aus.)
brother round mouth [early 19C]
bucket [1930s+] (US)
bum [late 18C+]
bumbo [late 18C+]
bum-fiddle [early 18C]
bumhole [mid-19C+]
bung [late 18C+]
butt pussy [20C] (US gay)
camera obscura [late 19C-1900s] (US; Latin 'a dark place')
catflap [1990s]
chuff [1940s+]
cigar burn [1990s]
crack [1960s+]
date [1910s+] (Aus./N.Z.)
deadeye [late 18C-1900s]
dot [1950s+] (Aus.)
eye of one's arse [20C] (Irish)
fifth point of contact [1990s] (US; a woman's anus, the
     other four 'points' being the mouth, nipples and vagina)
flipside [1980s+] (US gay)

THE ANUS IN RHYMING SLANG

rhyming with *arsehole*
  elephant and castle [late 19C+]
  Windsor castle [20C]
rhyming with *shitter* or *shiter*
  council gritter [1990s]
  Gary Glitter [1990s]
  ronson [1990s]
rhyming with *jacksie*
  London taxi [20C]
rhyming with *hole*
  merry old soul [20C]
  north pole [20C]
  south pole [20C]
rhyming with *ring*
  pearly king [20C]

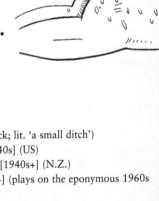

freckle [1960s+] (Aus.)
gazoo [20C]
gee-gee [1950s+] (US)
gig/giggy [20C] (Can.)
golden rivet [1940s+]
gripples [20C] (US Black; lit. 'a small ditch')
grommet [late 19C-1940s] (US)
gunga/gonga/gunger [1940s+] (N.Z.)
Hawaiian eye [1970s+] (plays on the eponymous 1960s
    TV programme)
jack [late 19C+]

jacksie [late 19C+]
jampot [1970s+] (US Black)
kazoo [1960s+]
keister [1930s+] (US; German *Kiste*, a box)
kite [20C] (Irish; dial. 'the stomach')
leather [1940s+] (US)
lolly [1960s] (US)
monocular eyeglass [mid-late 19C]
moon [mid-18C+]
mustard pot [1940s-50s] (US)
red-eye [1950s+]
rinctum [20C] (US Black)
rissole [1970s+] (Aus.)
rosebud [1950s-60s] (US gay)
roundeye [1950s+]
rusty bullet wound [1990s]
rusty sheriff's badge
rusty washer [1990s]
satchel [19C] (US)
third eye [20C] (US)
tradesman's/tradesman's entrance [1990s]
trap two/number two [1990s]
wazoo [20C] (US)
where the monkey shoves his nuts [late 19C+]
windmill [early 19C]
workman's entrance [1990s] (i.e. 'the back door')
ying-yang [1960s+]
you know where [20C]

THE HOLE

arsehole [19C+]
arsle/assle [20C]
batcave [1970s-80s] (gay)
batty-hole [20C] (W.I.)
blowhole [1940s]
bunghole [17C; 1930s+]
butthole [1950s+] (US)
cornhole [1910s+] (orig. US)
ding [1950s+] (Aus.; lit. 'a hole')
dinger [1930s+] (Aus.)
dukie hole [1970s+] (US Black; *dukie* = excrement)
hole [late 14C+]
porthole [17C]
quoit [1940s+] (Aus.)
ring [late 19C+]
ringpiece [late 19C+]
ringtail [20C]
round mouth [early 19C]
round pussy [20C] (US)
shithole [19C+]

THE ROAD, TUBE, TUNNEL OR PIPE

cackpipe [1990s]
chute [1970s+] (US)
dirt-chute [1940s+] (US)
dirt road [1910s+]
dirt track [1960s+]
flue [20C]

fudge tunnel [1990s]
Grand Canyon [1960s+] (US gay)
heinie highway [20C] (US; *heinie* = 'hind end')
Lincoln Tunnel [1960s+] (US gay)
loon pipe [1990s]
mustard road [1970s+] (US)
pooh chute [1990s]
poop-chute [20C]
road less travelled [1990s]
rocky road [20C] (US)
shit-chute [20C]
tan track [late 19C+]
tewel/tuel [late 14C] (lit. 'a pipe')

120 THE SOURCE OF EXCREMENT

ballinocack [late 18C-early 19C] (Irish; lit. 'shit town')
crapper [1920s+] (orig. US)
dilberry creek [mid-late 19C]
dilberry-maker [mid-late 19C]
dirt box [20C]
fart box [1960s+] (US)
fugo [17C-18C] (*fogo* = the smell of breaking wind)
shit-box [1990s]
shiter [1950s+]
shitter [20C] (US)
spice island [early-mid-19C]
stank [1970s+] (US Black)
stench-trench [20C]
tar pit (US)
winker-stinker [1960s+] (US prison)

A BOX OF CHOCOLATES

Bourneville boulevard [1990s]
Cadbury channel [1990s]
choccy [1990s]
chocolate eye [1990s]
chocolate highway [1970s+] (US)
chocolate runway [1990s]
chocolate starfish [1990s]
chocolate tea-towel holder [1990s]
chocolate whizzway [1990s]
coco [1990s]
Hershey highway [1970s+] (US)

121

'BROWN' TERMS

Bovril bypass [1990s]
Bovril hornpipe [1990s]
bronza/bronzer/bronzo [1950s+] (Aus.)
bronze [1920s+] (Aus.)
bronze eye [1990s]
brown bullethole [1990s]
brown eye [1970s+]
brownie [1920s+] (US)
brown pipe [1990s]
brown star/starfish [1990s]
brown trail [mid-20C+]
khaki buttonhole [1990s]
old brown windsor [1920s+] (Aus.)

THE BOTTOM OR BUTTOCKS

acre/acher [20C] (Aus.; i.e. a broad expanse)
afternoon [20C] (W.I.)
antipodes [mid-19C-1920s] (the 'bottom' of the world)
arse/ass [17C+]
ashcan [1910s] (US)
assbone [1970s] (US)
axle [1930s-50s] (i.e. 'underneath' a vehicle)
bahakas [1950s+] (US)
bam-bam [20C] (W.I.)
bamsie/bamsee/bamsey [20C] (W.I.)
baseburner [late 19C] (US)
bat-bat [20C] (W.I. juv.)
bati/batti/batty [1910s+] (W.I.)
bazooka [1950s+]
bertiss [1940s+] (W.I.)
bim [1930s-40s]
binky [20C] (US)
bird dog [20C] (US)
biscuits [1930s+] (orig. US Black)
blind Cupid [late 18C]
blind eye [late 18C-1900s]
bohunkus/bohunky [1940s+] (US)
bombosity [20C] (US)
booty [1920s+] (US Black)
bot/bott [1920s+]
botsie [20C] (W.I.)
bottie/botty [mid-19C+]
boungie/boongy bungee [20C] (W.I.)
box [1960s] (US Black)

b.t.m. [1910s+] (i.e. 'bottom')
bubblebutt [1980s+] (US campus; refers to large buttocks)
bucket [20C] (US)
bum [late 18C+]
bumba/bumpa [20C] (US Black)
bumbazine/bombazine [mid-19C] (US)
bumbo [late 18C+]
bumbosity [20C] (US)
bumkin [late 18C]
bumper [20C] (US)
bumper kit [1990s] (US Black)
bumpy [20C] (US)
bun [1950s-70s]
bunchy [1940s+] (W.I.)
bundie [20C] (Irish)
bung [1960s+] (US)
bunghole [1960s+] (US)
bunny [1930s+] (US; i.e. the rabbit's 'tail')
buns [1960s+]
bustle [1920s-70s] (US)
butt [mid-19C+]
butter [1980s+] (US Black)
cakes [1960s] (US)
can [late 19C+]
case o' pistles [20C] (Ulster)
cheeks [early 17C; 1920s+]
chinstrap [1910s+]
chips [1950s+] (US)
chuff [1940s+]
corybungo/corybungus
    [early 19C]

cracker [late 17C-18C]
crapper [1920s+] (orig. US)
crupper [late 16C]
cupcakes [1980s+] (US gay)
cushions [20C] (US)
daniel [1930s-40s] (US Black)
date [1910s+] (Aus./N.Z.)
dingaling [1950s+] (Aus.)
dinger [1930s+] (Aus.)
dish [1950s+] (gay)
do-nothing stool [1970s] (US Black)
dopey [late 18C]
double jugg/juggs [late 17C-19C]
doughy [1950s] (Aus.)
duff [late 19C+]
duffus [1940s] (US)
dumbarton/dumby [1910s] (W.I.)
duster [1940s+] (US Black)
dusty behind [1980s+] (US Black)
Dutch dumplings [1950s-70s]
English muffins [1960s+] (US gay)
fanny [1920s+] (US)
fart box [20C]
feak [early 19C]
fern [1950s+] (US)
frances [20C] (US; i.e. 'fanny')
full moon [1970s+]
fun [late 17C-18C]
glutes [1980s+] (US; i.e. *gluteus maximus*)
goat [mid-19C]
gogo [20C] (US)

....

THE BOTTOM IN RHYMING SLANG

rhyming with *arse*
    aristotle [late 19C+]
    arris [20C] (= aristotle = bottle and glass = arse)
    bottle and glass [20C] (Aus.)
    Khyber/Khyber Pass [1940s+]
    looking glass [1960s] (US)
rhyming with *bum*
    fife and drum [mid-20C]
    kingdom come [1970s]
    pipe and drum [20C]
    rumdadum [1910s-20s]
    tom thumb/tom [20C]
rhyming with *tail*
    Daily Mail [1930s+]

....

gooseberry grinder [late 18C-19C]
Greek side [1930s+] (*Greek* = homosexual)
grumper [1970s] (US)
guava [1970s+] (S.Afr.; from the shape of the fruit)
heinie [1910s+] (US; i.e. 'hind end')
hockey box [1970s-80s] (US)
hoochie-pap [1920s] (US Black)
hot buns [1980s+] (US gay)
Hottentots [20C] (from the nakedness of African
    tribespeople)
huff [late 19C]
jibs [1950s+] (US Black; lit. 'a protruding sail')

johnson [1980s]

jubilee [late 19C] (coined at the time of Queen Victoria's Golden Jubilee in 1887, i.e. the 'arse-end' of the century)

juff [late 19C+] (French *joue*, 'a cheek')

jumbo [1940s+] (N.Z.)

jutland [19C] (it 'juts out')

keel [late 19C+]

keister [1930s+] (US; German *Kiste*, a box)

labonza [1950s+] (US; Ital. *la pancia*, the paunch)

money-maker [1960s+] (US)

moon [mid-18C+]

muffins [1960s+] (US gay)

naf/naff [mid-19C] (backslang; *fan* = fanny)

nancy [early 19C]

nennen [20C] (W.I.; from a word in the Twi language of West Africa meaning 'to defecate')

nockandro [17C-mid-18C] (ext. of *nock*, the 'cleft' of the buttocks)

parking place [20C]

part that goes over the fence last [late 19C] (US)

patootie/patoot [1920s+] (US)

peaches [1980s+] (US gay)

pooper [1950s+]

prat [16C+]

quoit [1940s+] (Aus.)

rass [1940s+] (W.I.)

roby douglas [late 18C] (a person 'with one eye and a stinking breath')

royal [20C] (W.I./Trin.)

rusty-dusty [1930s-50s] (US)

rydim [1940s] (W.I.; i.e. the 'rhythm' of moving buttocks)

satchel [19C] (US)
scut [late 16C+] (*scut* = rabbit's tail)
seat of honour/shame/vengeance [19C]
seats [1940s-50s]
sit-me-down [1920s+]
sitting room [late 19C-1900s]
sit-upon [mid-19C]
southern can [1930s-50s] (US Black)
squatter [20C]
Sunday face [19C] (plays on *Sunday face*,
    i.e. a sanctimonious expression)
sweetcakes [1980s+] (US gay)
sweetcheeks [1980s+] (US gay)
thunderbox [20C] (US)
toby [late 17C-mid-19C]
toches [20C] (Yiddish)
tooshie [1930s+] (US)
tush [late 19C+]
two fat cheeks/and ne'er a nose [18C]
ultimatum [early 19C]
wazoo [20C] (US)
Westphalia [late 19C-1920s] (puns on *Westphalia* ham,
    the upper thigh)
winkie [1970s+] (US)

'THE BEHIND'

abaft the wheel-house [late 19C] (US)
ampersand [19C] ('&' appeared at the *end* of the alphabet
    in 19C nursery alphabets)
back-land [late 17C-mid-19C] (W.I.)

back-porch [1950+] (US)
backside [late 18C+]
behind [late 18C+]
caboose [19C] (US)
dummock [19C] (Romani *dummock*, the back)
end [1990s] (US Black teen)
hind [1930s-40s] (US Black)
hinder end/parts/world [19C+]
hinder entrance [19C]
hinders [late 19C-1930s]
hindside [20C]
hinterland [late 19C]
Netherlands [18C]
poop [early 17C] (the 'rear seat')
posteriors/posterior [early 17C+]
rear [late 18C+]
rear end [1930s+] (orig. US)
rearview [1980s]
stern [early 17C+]
tail [early 18C+]
tailbone [20C] (US)
truck-end [1910s]

THE PERINEUM

chin rest [1990s] (in the context of a man performing
    oral sex on a woman)
Finsbury bridge [1990s]
piffin bridge [1990s]

Turned On

LUST AND DESIRE

dog [1960s+] (US Black)
horn [late 18C+]
the hornies [1970s+] (US)
hot nuts [1930s+] (US)
hot pants [1920s+] (US)
hot rocks [1940s+] (US)
the hots [1940s+]
itch [17C+]
letch [1940s+] (orig. US)
nasties [20C] (US Black)
notion [late 19C+] (Irish)
rush of blood to the crutch [1930s+]
the stonies [1970s+]
    (US; *stones* = testicles)
zazzle [1930s-60s]
    (US Black)

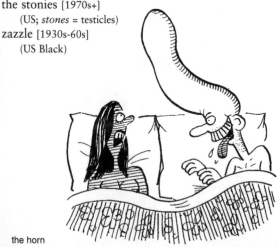

the horn

SEXY

babelicious [1990s]
bacon [1990s] (US campus; *bacon* = penis)
bed-worthy [1930s+]
candy [20C] (US; i.e. a sexually desirable person)
cunty [19C+]
down and dirty [1980s+] (orig. US)
foxy [1910s+] (orig. US)
fuckable [late 19C]
fuck-me [1980s+]
fucksome [late 19C] (of a woman)
ginchy [1950s+] (*ginch* = vagina)
hairy [mid-19C+]
hootchy-kootchy [late 19C+] (orig. US)
horny [late 19C+]
hot [14C+]
juicy [late 19C+]
nasty [mid-19C] (orig. US)
oomphy [1950s+] (US)
red-hot [1900s-30s] (US)
skanky/scankie [1970s+]
    (US Black; *skank* = a promiscous woman)
spunky [1960s+] (Aus.)
steamy [1960s+] (orig. US)
twisty [20C] (US; i.e. having a curvy body)
warm [late 19C+] (US)
warm as they make them [late 19C]
zazzy [1930s-60s] (US Black)

TO EXCITE

bring on [20C]
come over at [1910s-20s] (orig. US)
do things to/for [1930s+]
fire up [1970s+] (orig. US Black/campus)
give someone rocks [1950s+] (US; *rocks* = sexual desire)
have someone's nose open [1950s+] (US Black;
    i.e. cause heavy breathing)
prime someone's pump [1950s+]
pump [1950s+] (US teen)
steam [1950s+] (orig. US; i.e. to 'get all steamed up')
turn on [1960s+]

TO FEEL SEXUALLY EXCITED

bust a sweat [1980s+] (US Black)
come over all unnecessary [1930s+]
cream in one's jeans [1960s+]
feel gay [19C-1910s] (*gay* = sexy)
have an aching tooth [16C]
have an itch in the belly [mid-17C-late 19C]
have eyes for [1930s+] (US)
have hot pants [1920s+] (orig. US)
have one's mind in the mud [1900s-40s] (US Black)
have red-eye for [20C] (W.I.)
have the hots for [1940s+] (orig. US)
look with red-eye/red-eye at [20C] (W.I.)
make a pass [1920s+] (orig. US)
put one's eye on [20C] (W.I.)

red one's eye for [20C] (W.I.)
red-eye after [20C] (W.I.)
skin catch fire/fire for [20C] (W.I.)

THE SEXUAL LOOK

aspect [late 19C-1900s]
bedroom eyes [1950s+]
fuck-me eyes [1980s] (US)
goo-goo eyes [20C]
googy eyes [1910s-20s] (US)
ogle [late 17C+]
sweet-eye [20C] (W.I.)

133

FEELING AROUSED

after one's greens [late 19C+] (*greens* = intercourse)
led by the head of one's dick [1990s] (US Black)
burners on high [1990s] (US campus)
chucked [early 19C] (UK Und.)
doggy [20C] (US Black)
freakish [1940s-50s] (US Black)
freaky [1970s+] (US)
fruity [20C]
fuckish [late 19C]
horned-up [1960s+] (US)
horn-mad [late 18C-19C]
horny [late 19C+]
horsey [20C] (lit. 'yearning')
hot [14C+]
hot as/hotter than a fresh-fucked fox in a forest fire
    [1950s+] (US)
hot for [1940s+] (orig. US)
humpty [20C]

FEELING FRUSTRATED

blue balls [20C]
fuckstrated [1980s+] (US campus)
goaty [1910s-50s] (US)
hogged up [1990s]
night starvation [1940s]
Swedish headache [1960s+] (US)

hungry [1970s+] (US campus)
mashy [late 19C]
nutty/nutty upon [early-mid-19C]
open [1950s+] (US Black)
pass in the pot [late 19C-1900s] (rhy. sl. 'hot')
prime [19C]
proud [late 17C-19C]
purse-proud [late 17C-18C]
randy [late 18C+]
rooty [20C] (US; *root* = intercourse)
rusty [late 19C+] (Aus.)
sexed up [20C]
steamed up [1920s+]
wide-open [1980s+] (US Black)

THE SEXUALLY EXCITED WOMAN

begging for it [1950s+]
dripping for it/dripping for it like a butcher's
    daughter [1920+] (orig. Aus.)
gagging for it [1980s+]
fizzing at the bung [1990s]
fizzing at the bunghole [1990s]
fizzing at the slit [1990s]
juiced/juiced up [1970s+] (US)
on for one's greens [mid-19C+] (*greens* = intercourse)
on heat [late 19C+]
screamer and creamer [1970s+]
wet [mid-18C+]

PROMISCUOUS

fass [20C] (US Black)
fast [early 19C+]
flash [early-mid-19C]
fly [late 19C]
fresh and fast/forward [20C] (W.I.)
fuck-nutty [1940s]
fuck-struck [1960s]
fucky [20C]
gay in the arse [18C] (*gay* = forward)
hot as a fire-cracker [1910s+] (Can.)
hot in the tail [late 17C-early 18C]
hot to trot [1950s+]

FLIRTS AND TEASES

ball-buster [1970s+]
cockchafer [late 19C]
cockteaser/c.t. [late 19C+]
gill-flirt [17C-19C]
jilt [late 17C-mid-19C]
pricktease [1950s+]
prickteaser/p.t. [1950s+]
scammer [1980s+] (US campus; lit. a 'confidence trickster')
spoon [mid-19C] (i.e. 'open and shallow')
tease [1970s+]
teaser [late 19C+]
trap [1980s+] (US campus)

light in the tail [late 17C-early 18C]
rammish/rammy [late 18C-early 19C]
roundheeled [1920s+] (US)
slaggy [1970s+]
swinging [1960s+]
tomming [1930s+] (*tom* = a whore)
tramp-ass [1970s] (US Black)
trampish ass [1970s] (US Black)
warm in the tail [late 17C-early 18C]

TO BE PROMISCUOUS

bedhop [1960s+]
dick around [1940s+]
dog around [20C]
fool around [1970s+]
fuck a duck [1930s+]
fuck around [1930s+]
hawk one's pearly [1970s+]
screw around [1930s+]
   (orig. US)
shoot the thrill [1970s]
   (US Black)
sleep around [1920s+]
   (orig. US)

137

THE PROMISCUOUS PERSON

bed/bedroom athlete [1940s+] (orig. US)
boogie [1950s] (US Black)
cum-freak [1960s+]
frog [1990s] (they'll 'hop' into bed with anyone)
fuckaholic [1980s+]
hosebeast [1990s] (US)
hose monster [1980s] (US)
hottie [1990s] (US black)
mucky pup [20C] (Aus.)
player [1950s+] (orig. US Black)
tickle-pitcher [late 17C-18C]

138 THE PROMISCUOUS MAN

beard-jammer [1920s+] (US)
belly bumper [19C]
bird's-nester [19C]
boudoir bandicoot [1980s] (Aus.)
bum-faker [18C]
bum-ranger [18C]
bum-shaver [18C]
bum-tickler [18C]
bum-worker [18C]
bun-duster [1920s] (US)
buttonhole worker [19C]
cassa [1940s+] (Aus.; abbr. 'Casanova')
charity [1960s+] (Aus. gay; 'he gives it away for free')
chauverer-cove [mid-19C]
chauvering-cove [mid-19C]

chippy-chaser [early 19C+] (i.e. a devotee of prostitutes)
clapster [19C+] (i.e. one who risks 'the clap')
cock of the game [19C]
dog [1950s+] (US Black)
fishmonger [17C] (*fish* = vagina)
fuckster [late 17C+]
goat [late 17C+]
gulley-/gully-raker [19C]
hair-monger [late 19C+]
he'd fuck anything with a hole in it [20C]
high priest of Paphos [19C] (*Paphos*, birthplace of Venus)
ho/hoe [1980s+] (US Black)
horseman [18C+]
hustler [1970s+] (US campus)
jazzhound [1920s] (US; *jazz* = to have sex)
jelly bean [1920s-50s] (US)
john among the maids [19C]
judy-slayer [late 19C]
jumbler [17C-18C]
killer-diller [1930s+] (orig. US)
king of clubs [19C] (*club* = penis)
knocker [17C]
ladies' tailor [19C]
leg-lifter [early 18C-late 19C]
leg man [1970s] (US campus)
linen-lifter [1980s] (Aus.)
lounge lizard [1910s+]
love machine [1970s+] (US)
lusty-guts [16C]
lusty lawrence [16C]
make-out artist [1930s+] (US)

he gets more ass than a toilet seat [1940s+] (orig. US)
Mormon [19C] (US; from the sect's polygamy)
Mr Horner [19C] (a play on 'whore')
muttoner [late 17C-early 19C]
mutton-monger [early 16C-early 18C]
niggler [17C-late 18C]
performer [late 19C-1900s]
poodle-faker [20C] (the poodle as a woman's
    fashionable pet)
ram [1930s+]
rattle cap [mid-19C]
rider [18C+]
rogue [1960s+] (US Black)
servant [19C]
sex machine [1960s+]
sharpshooter [19C+]
skirt-chaser [1940s+] (orig. US)
sportsman [19C]
Stavin Chain [1900s-20s] (US Black; from the hero of a
    popular ballad)
sweetback/sweetback man
    [1900s-60s] (US Black)
tea-hound [1920s] (US)
tough cat [1950s+] (US Black)
town bull [late 17C-19C]
village ram [1930s+] (W.I.)
warm member [19C]

YOU'RE ONLY AFTER ONE THING

THE PROMISCUOUS WOMAN

alley bat [20C] (US)

alley cat [1920s+] (US)

amorosa [early 17C-early 18C] (lit. 'amorous woman')

bag [late 19C+] (US)

baggage [16C+]

banbury [late 19C-1910s] ('she rides a cock horse to
    Banbury Cross')

barber's chair [18C] ('used by all-comers')

bat [early 17C-early 19C]

bicycle [1940s+] (everyone can 'ride' her)

biff [1920s+] (US campus)

biffer [1920s+] (US Black)

bike [1940s+]

blister [1960s]

box-about [1950s] (W.I.)

brim [late 17C-mid-19C]

bug [20C] (US)

bum [1920s+] (US)

bunny [20C] (US Black)

butter [1980s+] (US Black; *butter* = vagina)

carrion-hunter [late 18C-mid-19C]

charity cunt [1940s+] (US)

charity dame [1930s+] (Aus.)

charity girl [20C] (US)

charity worker [1940s+] (US)

chickenhead [1960s+] (US Black)

chip [late 19C-1950s] (US)

cleaver [late 18C-early 19C]

cubba [1940s+] (W.I.)
daffy [late 19C]
dame [mid-19C+] (mainly US)
dickhound [1980s+] (US Black)
dildo [1990s] (Irish)
dirtbag [1940s+] (orig. US)
dirty Gertie [1920s-40s] (US)
dirty leg [1960s+] (US)
dirty neck [1910s-60s] (US)
dragon [17C-19C]
easy mort [mid-17C-early 18C]
fanfoot [20C] (US Black; lit. 'flaunt-foot')
flap [early-mid-17C]
freak [1960s+] (US Black)
fruit [1910s-30s]
garden tool [1990s] (US campus; *ho* or *hoe* = prostitute)
goer [1950s+]
good-time Jane [1940s-60s] (US)
grubber [19C]
hank [1980s+] (US campus)
high-flyer/-flier [late 17C-19C; US 20C]
highty-tighty/heighty-toity [late 17C-late 18C]
hobby horse [late 16C-early 17C] (free to be 'ridden')
hogmanay [19C]
hoity-toity [early 18C-early 19C]
hoozie/hosie [1970s] (US)
horns-to-sell [18C-mid-19C] (specifically a promiscuous
    wife; *horns* = cuckoldry)
hose [1980s+] (US campus)
hosebag [1970s] (orig. US campus)
hose queen [1980s+] (US campus)

hot beef [19C]
hot-bot/lady hot-bot [20C]
hot meat [19C]
hot mutton [19C]
hot box [1930s-60s] (US)
hot pot [1920s-30s] (US Black)
hyperdrive whore [1980s+] (US campus)
jagabat [20C] (W.I.; Hindi 'sweet talk')
jamette [20C] (W.I.; Fr. sl. *jeanette*, a whore)
jing-bang [1940s+] (W.I.)
judy [19C+] (orig. Und.)
jump [1930s-40s] (US)
kite [late 19C-1950s] (US; lit. 'a bird of prey')
knock [16C; 20C]
lay [1930s+]
leather [mid-16C+]
leg [1940s+] (US)
leggo-beast [1940s+] (W.I.; lit. 'wild beast')
letching-piece [20C]
lift skirts [mid-19C]
light heels [early 18C-19C]
Little Miss Roundheels [1950s+] ('she's always falling on
    her back')
long-eye [20C] (W.I.)
lossie [1950s+] (S.Afr.; 'a loose one')
lowheel [1930s-60s]
lowie [1930s-60s]
low rent [1960s+] (US campus)
lust dog [1970s+] (US campus)
make [1940s+] (orig. US)
mat [1940s] (US)

mattressback [1960s+] (US)
Melvyn Bragg [1990s] (rhy. sl. 'shag')
mole [1950s+] (Aus./N.Z.)
moll [late 16C+]
mount [1970s+] (US Black)
mustard [1920s+] (i.e. 'hot stuff')
mutton [early 16C+]
notch [1910s+] (US)
owl-gal [1940s] (W.I.)
pheasant [late 17C-early 19C]
pig [1960s+] (US campus)
pig meat [late 19C-1940s] (US Black)
pintle-fancier [early 19C-1900s] (*pintle* = penis)
pintle-ranger [early 19C-1900s]
pitch [1970s+] (US campus)
player [1960s+] (N.Z.)
plover [17C]
poke [late 19C+]
psycho hose beast [1980s]
pump [1970s+]
punch [1970s+] (US campus)
punchboard [1950s+] (US campus)
puta [1950s+] (US Sp. 'whore')
rag [late 19C] (Aus.)
rattler [1920s]
rig [late 16C-late 19C]
right sort [20C]
rig mutton [mid-late 16C]
rigsby [mid-16C-late 17C] (lit. 'one who plays the wanton')
road whore [1980s+] (US campus)
roundheel [1920s+] (US)

sack-chaser [1990s] (US Black)
Sal slappers [late 19C] (lit. 'Sally the Slapper')
scrubber [1950s+]
scuzzbag [1970s+] (US)
shickster [mid-19C]
short-heeled wench [late 18C-early 19C]
short heels [late 18C-early 19C]
skeeza/skeeger/skeezer [1980s+] (orig. US Black;
    lit. 'frolicker')
slack [1950s+] (W.I.)
slag [1950s+] (lit. a 'slack person')
slapper [1970s+]
sleaze [1980s+] (US campus)
sleazo [1980s+] (US campus)
sleazoid [1980s+] (US campus)
sleepytime girl [1950s+] (US)
slorch [1990s] (US campus; from *sl*ut + wh*or*e + bit*ch*)
slusher [1990s] (she is always damp with desire)
slut-puppy [1980s+] (US campus)
snot [1980s+]
soap [late 19C-1900s]
spunk-bucket [1990s]
spunk-dustbin [1990s]
stinker [1990s]
stoinker [1990s]
strawberry [1980s+] (US teen; *strawberry* = a bruise;
    i.e. the woman has a scarred back or knees from
    constant intercourse or fellatio)
streetcleaner [1930s-50s] (US Black)
strum [late 17C-18C]
sweat hog [1970s+] (US campus)

tart [late 19C+]

teazy-whacker [20C] (Irish; *teazle* = vagina)

third-legger [1980s+] (US Black)

thoroughfare [1930s] (US Black)

thorough good-natured wench [late 18C-early 19C]

three-way woman [1990s] (US; i.e. she permits vaginal, oral and anal penetration)

thrill [1950s+] (Irish)

tickle-tail [late 15C-late 18C]

tickle-toby [late 17C-19C]

town bicycle [1920s+] (orig. Aus.)

town bike [1940s+]

town pump [1970s+]

town punch [1970s+]

tramp [1920s+] (orig. US)

turtle [20C] (orig. Aus.; 'once she's on her back, she's fucked')

twigger [mid-16C-late 17C]

two-bit hustler [20C]

wagtail [late 17C-18C]

wajan/wajang/wajank [20C] (W.I.; lit. 'wait, John')

walk-up fuck [20C] (Aus.; a man needs only to walk up and ask)

wench [1980s+] (US campus)

what-shall-call-um [early-mid-19C]

whore [1970s+]

whoredog [1980s+] (US campus)

zipper [1930s] (US)

MATING CALLS

Man to woman – positive

do fries go with that shake? [1980s+]

doog gels [mid 19C+] (backslang, 'good legs')

next time you make a pie will you give me
a piece? [late 19C-1910s] (Can.)

wanna do a thing? [1960s] (US Black)

whap that thing! [1960s-70s] (US Black)

Man to man – positive

been there [late 19C] (i.e. the speaker has already
enjoyed the woman in question)

I could fuck the arse off that [1950s+]

I wouldn't kick her out of bed [20C]

please mother open the door [late 19C] (i.e. so that
the speaker can meet the passing beauty)

she can sit on my face any day [1940s+]

Man to man – negative

don't fancy yours [20C]

mind the paint [late 19C] (i.e. the woman is wearing
too much make-up)

wouldn't touch it with a 40-foot bargepole [20C]

147

Sex for One

MASTURBATION

arming the cannon [1990s]
bashing [late 19C+]
bat [1940s+] (Aus.)
beat-off [1970s] (US)
blanket drill [1930s+]
couch hockey for one [1990s]
diddle [mid-19C+]
dishonourable discharge [1960s+]
do-it-yourself [1950s+]
dusting the duvet [1990s]
engaging sixth gear [1990s] (mutual masturbation in
    the front seat of a parked car)
frig [late 18C-late 19C]
frigging [late 16C+]
grind [late 19C+]
gusset typing [1990s] (of a woman)
hard labour [1990s]
Harry Johnson [1990s] (i.e. 'hand job')
herkin the gherkin [20C]
Irish promotion [20C] (gay)
Irish wedding/wedding [20C] (gay)
jack-off [1930s+] (US)
jacking off [20C]
jerk-off [1920s+] (US)
jerking [late 19C+]
jerking off the jelly juice [1990s]
j.o. scene [1960s] (i.e. jerk-off)
kit-kat shuffle [1990s] (of a woman; kitty = vagina)
larking [19C]

lonely art [20C]

mary ellen [1940s+] (US)

much goo about nothing [1990s]

night exercises [1990s]

number three [20C] (on the model of the juv. terms
    number one and *number two*)

the old one-two [20C]

Onan's Olympics [19C] (the biblical *Onan* 'cast his seed
    upon the ground')

one-eye target practice [1990s]

one-gun salute [1990s]

one-legged race [1970s]

one-man show [1990s]

one-stick drum improvisation [20C]

pocket pool [1950s+]

Portuguese pump [1950s]

pud wrestling [1950s+] (US)

rub-off [19C+]

rub-up [19C+]

sailor's joy [20C]

single dingles [1990s]

soldier's joy [mid-19C-1900s]

squirt 'n' spurt [1990s] (US)

toss [late 18C+]

toss-off [mid-18C+]

tug [1950s+]

unloading [1990s]

wank [1940s+]

wanking [late 19C+]

waz/wazz [1970s+]

yankee [1950s] (gay)

MASTURBATION: SPECIALITIES

chain jerk [1930s+] (US; masturbation by a group
of boys in a circle)

circle jerk [1950s+] (orig. US; masturbation by a
group of boys in a circle)

diddy ride [1990s] (i.e. by placing the penis between
a woman's breasts)

docking [1980s+] (US; a form of gay mutual masturbation involving the drawing of one's man's foreskin
over the glans of the other man's penis)

Dutch fuck [1990s] (US; i.e. by placing the penis
between a woman's breasts)

French fuck/wank [1990s] (i.e. by placing the penis
between a woman's breasts)

fucksock [1990s] (a sock used as a repository for
semen during masturbation)

gob and rub [1960s] (refers to spitting on the penis
before masturbation)

housewife's hour [1960s+] (US gay; the afternoon
as a time for masturbation)

jack bumps [1960s+] (US; acne supposedly caused
by masturbation)

posh wank [1990s] (masturbating while wearing a
condom)

pulling party [1970s] (US; group masturbation)

rubberneck [1970s] (US Black; also means 'to self-fellate')

shower spank [1980s+] (US teen; to masturbate
in the shower)

Swedish [1960s+] (mutual masturbation)

titty fuck [1990s] (US; i.e. by rubbing the penis
between a woman's breasts)

USING THE HAND

button finger [1990s] (i.e. the finger a woman uses to
  masturbate herself)
dry-mouthed widow [1960s+] (i.e. the hand, rather than
  the vagina, as the place for the penis)
finger blasting [1990s]
five against one [20C]
five on one [20C]
five-finger solo [1990s]
five-finger/-knuckle shuffle [1990s]
five-fingered exercise [1970s+]
five-fingered widow [1970s+]
fly fishing [1990s]
four-fingered shuffle [1980s+]
four sisters on thumb street [1970s+] (US Black)
hand fucking [1960s+] (US Black)
hand gallop [1970s]
hand job [1960s+]
hand gig [1960s+] (gay)
hand jig [1930s-60s] (US prison)
hand job [1930s+] (US)
hand shandy [20C]
hand-to-gland combat [20C]
hand/han solo [1990s]
hand/handy work [20C]
knuckle shuffle [1990s]
lady/old lady five fingers [20C]
manual labour [1990s]
manual override [1990s]

Mary Fist [1940s+] (US)
Mary Five-fingers [1940s+] (US)
Mary Palm [1940s+] (US)
Minnie Five Fingers [1920s] (US)
Miss Fist [20C]
Mother Fist and her Five Daughters [20C]
Mother Five Fingers [20C]
Mr Palmer and his five sons [1950s+]
Mrs Palm/Mrs Palmer and her Five Daughters
    [1950s+]
one off the wrist [1970s+]
paw-paw tricks [19C]
widow five-finger [20C]
wrist aerobics [1990s]
wrist marathon [1990s]

154

MASTURBATION IN RHYMING SLANG

rhyming with *wank*

Allied Irish [1990s] (Irish; i.e. Allied Irish Bank)
Barclay's [1930s+] (i.e. Barclay's Bank)
donkey spanking [1980s+]
ham shank [1990s]
J. Arthur [1940s+] (i.e. J. Arthur Rank)
Jodrell [1950s+] (i.e. Jodrell Bank)
piggy bank [20C]
Sherman [1940s+] (i.e. Sherman tank)
Yorkshire penny bank [20C]

TO MASTURBATE: THE MAN

address congress [1990s] (US)
appropriate the means [1980s+]
audition the finger puppets [1980s+]
ball off [20C]
be your own best friend [1990s]
bequeath one's genes [1990s]
bleed the weed [1990s]
bliff [1990s]
bloat the vein [1990s]
blow one's dust [1960s-70s]
blow one's own horn [1990s]
bone it off [1990s]
bring off by hand [early 19C+]
bring oneself off [1960s+]
buck the bone [1990s]
burp the baby [1990s]
chafe at the bit [1990s]
charge the rod [1990s]
chong your schlong [1990s]
claw [19C]
climb mount baldy [1990s]
climb the tree [20C]
clobber the Kleenex [1990s]
close the deal [1990s]
come into your own [1980s+]
come to grips with yourself [1990s]
consult Dr Jerkoff [20C] (US)
converse with Harry Palm [1990s]
crank one's/the shank [20C]

create an arch [1990s]
crown the king [1990s]
cruise for an oozing [1990s]
dance with johnnie one-eye [1980s+]
dash one's doodle [19C]
date Rosy Palm and her sisters/five sisters [20C]
diddle [mid-19C+] (orig. US)
diddle the dinky [1980s+]
dig for change [1900s]
dinky one's slinky [1960s+]
drain Charles Dickens [1990s] (rhy. sl. 'choke the chicken')
drive the skin bus [1990s]
drool [1990s]
dub off [1910s] (US)
engage in safe sex [1980s+]
erupt Vesuvius [1990s]
examine the equipment [1990s]
express yourself [1980s+]
feel in one's pocket for one's
    big hairy rocket [20C]
fight the champ [1980s+]
file one's fun-rod [20C]
fire one's peter [20C]
firk the dude [20C]
fist fuck/fist [1960s]
fist one's mister [20C]
flay the emperor [1990s]
flip [late 19C+] (orig. Aus.)
flip off [1960s+]
freak off [1950s+] (US Black)
free the slaves [1990s]

LAY-LA

To Do . . .

a bathroom guitar solo [1990s]
a doodle-dandler [19C]
a dry waltz with oneself [1940s+]
a hand job [1960s+]
handiwork [1980s+]
it one's own/your way [1980s+]
one's nails [1980s+]
oneself off [1960s+]
the arm aerobics [1960s+]
the bachelor's shuffle [1980s+]
the backstroke roulette [1980s+]
the han solo [1980s+]
the hand jive/crazy hand jive [1960s]
the janitor thing [1990s] (i.e. it involves mopping
    the floor)
the pork sword jiggle [1990s]
the Portuguese pump [1990s]
the solitary rhumba [1990s]
the wash by hand [1970s+] (US)
the white knuckler [1990s]
your own thing [1980s+]

frig [late 16C+]
frig off [20C]
friggle [19C]
fuck Mrs Palmer [1990s]
fuck one's fist [20C]
fuck Palmela [1990s] (play on 'palm')

fuck without complications [1990s]
gallop one's/the antelope [mid-19C+]
give it a tug [1950s+]
give yourself a low five [1980s+]
give Yul Brynner a high five [1990s]
glop [1990s]
glue the lady's eyes shut [1990s]
go blind [20C]
go mingo [mid-19C]
go on a date with Handrea and Palmela [1990s]
go on a date with Rosy Palm and her five
   daughters [20C]
go on peewee's little adventure [1980s] (US)
go steady with one's right hand [1970s+] (US)
go to/come from Bangkok [1990s]
grab the flab/slab [1990s]

158

TO GET . . .

a grip on things [1990s]
comfortable [1990s]
in touch with one's inner self [1990s]
off [1970s+]
one's nuts off [1930s+] (orig. US Black)
one's pole varnished [1980s+]
one's rocks off [1960s+]
the dirty water off one's chest [20C]
the German soldier marching [1980s+]
to know yourself [1990s]

grease one's pole [1990s]
grind [1970s+]
grip the gold [1990s]
grip the pencil [1990s]
grip the tip [1990s]
hack one's mack [20C]
hand jive [1970s+] (US)
hand shandy [20C]
handle [19C]
hang the old man [20C]
haul one's own ashes [20C] (US)
hit on Rosy Palm [20C]
hitchhike to heaven [1990s]
hitchhike under the big top [1990s]
hold one's own [20C]
hold the bold [1990s]
hump one's hose [20C]
hump the horn [20C]
ignite the lightsaber [1980s+]
jack off [1930s+] (US)
jag off [1960s+] (US)
jerk [late 19C+]
jerk off [late 19C+]
jostle [1990s]
keep down the census [19C]
kill it [1990s]
kill off [1990s]
knock on wood [20C]
knock one out [1990s]
knock one's own thing [20C] (W.I./Belz.)
lark [19C]

To Have . . .

a ball [1940s+] (orig. US)
a big date with rosy palm [20C]
a conversation with the one-eyed trouser
    snake [1960s+]
a date with Fisty Palmer [1990s]
a taffy pulling contest [20C] (US)
a tug [1950s+] (Aus.)
a tug o' war with ol' cyclops [1990s]
a whack attack [1970s+]
an arm wrestle with your one-eyed vessel
    [1990s]
it off [1940s+]
oneself [1980s+] (US Black)
the urge for a surge [1990s]

And To Pull . . .

about [19C]
off [1960s+]
on peter [late 19C+]
one's joint [1930s+]
one's plonker [1910s+]
one's pud [1920s+] (orig. US)
one's wire [1970s+]
the chain [20C] (US)

160

lather a bar of soap [1920s-50s] (US)
let loose the juice [1990s]
lick the dick [1980s+]
lighten the load [1980s+]
massage the one-eyed monk [1990s]
meet Mary Palm and her five sisters [1950s+]
meet Rosie Hancock [1950s+]
meet with Mother Thumb and her daughters [20C]
meet your right-hand man [1990s]
mind one's own business [1990s]
negotiate a new contract [1990s]
pack one's palm [1990s]
pan for white gold [1990s]
pass math [1990s] (US)
perform a self-test [1980s+]
please one's pisser [20C]
pocket the rocket [1990s]
pop a wad/a wad by hand [20C]
pop one's cork [1960s+]
pop one's peter [1990s]
practise the Heimlich maneuver/manoeuvre [1990s]
prompt one's porpoise [20C]
prune the fifth limb [19C]
pump a gusher [1990s]
pump gas at the self-service island [1990s]
pump off [1950s+]
qualify in the testicular time trial [1990s]
rattle the bottle [1950s+] (US)
ride the great white knuckler [1990s]
ride the handcar [1940s+] (US)
ring one's dong [1990s]

rob the knob [1990s]
roll one's marbles [1950s] (US)
roll your own [1990s]
rub it up the wrong way [1990s]
rub off [19C]
rub the rod [20C]
rub up [19C+]

TO PLAY . . .

a flute solo on one's meat whistle [20C]
a little five-on-one [20C]
a lute solo [19C]
a one-stringed guitar [1990s]
a solo on one's meat whistle [1990s]
a tune on the one-holed flute [19C+]
an organ solo [1990s]
chopsticks [1960s+]
dolly up, dolly down, dolly sick [20C]
in a one-man show [1990s]
oneself off [18C-19C]
pocket billiards/pinball [1940s+]
solitaire [1990s]
tag with the pink torpedo [1990s]
the male organ [19C]
the skin flute [20C]
tug-o-war with the cyclops [1990s]
with oneself [1920s+]
with your willy wanker [1990s]

To Polish . . .

Charlie Brown [1980s+]
one's antlers [1980s+]
one's knob [1980s+]
one's sword [1980s+]
percy [1980s+]
the lighthouse [1980s+]
the penguin [1980s+]
the pole [1980s+]
the rocket [1980s+]
the sword [1980s+]
the viper [1980s+]
and gloss [20C]

163

run off a batch by hand [1990s]
run one's hand up the flagpole [20C]
salute the sailor [1990s]
sap one's woody [1990s]
scrape/cut one's horns [1960s+] (US)
screw off [20C] (US)
sew [1960s+] (US Black)
shag [1980s+]
shake [16C-1900s]
shake hands with Abraham Lincoln [1990s]
shake hands with the unemployed [1990s]
shake hands with the wife's best friend [1960s+]
shake the weasel [1990s]
shake up [19C]

shine one's pole [20C]
shine the barrel [1990s]
shine the helmet [1990s]
shoot for the moon [1990s]
shoot one's squirt [1990s]
shoot skeet [1990s]
shuffle the deck [1990s]
sing with rosie [1990s]
slap it [20C]
slap pappy [1990s]
slick one's stick [1990s]
slide the shaft [1990s]
slop out [1990s]
smack off [1990s]
snap one off [1990s]
snap the rubber [1990s]
spin one's own propellor [1960s+] (US)
spin the record [1990s]
spit one off [1990s]
spit-polish the purple helmet [1990s]
splash [1930s+]
spray the spectators [1990s]
spuff up [1990s]
squirt one off [1990s]
strain the main vein [1950s+]
strike the pink match [1960s+]
stroke one's oar [1970s] (US)
stroke/stroke it/off [1950s+]
strum the banjo [1990s]
summon the genie [1990s]
talk quietly to oneself [1990s]

TO MAKE . . .

a foreskin cone [1990s]
a rendezvous with Mrs Hand [1980s+]
a six-fist [1990s]
a solo flight [1990s]
fist-kabobs [1990s]
friends with Big Ed [1990s]
instant pudding [1990s]
out with yourself [1950s+] (US)
prick juice [1990s]
soup [1990s]
the bald man puke/sick [1990s]
the hooded cobra spit [1990s]
the rooster crow [1990s]
the scene with the magazine [1900s]

165

thrap/throp [1990s] (dial. *throp*, to beat or flog)
throw out [1990s]
tickle one's dick [20C]
tickle one's fancy [20C]
tickle one's pickle [20C]
tickle the ivory [1990s]
tonk [1910s+] (Aus.)
tootle one's flute [1980s+]
toss [mid-18C+]
toss it [20C]
toss off/toss oneself off [late 18C+]
touch oneself up [20C]

trim one's horn [1990s]
trim one's wick [1990s]
turn Japanese [1990s] (perh. because the eyes are half-closed during orgasm)
varnish one's pole [1980s+]
varnish the flagpole [1980s+]
visit Niagara Falls [20C] (*Niagara Falls* = balls)
visit Rosy Palm and her five daughters [20C]
wake the dead [1990s]
walk old one-eye [1990s]
wank [late 19C+]
wank off [20C]
wank the crank [1960s+]
wanker the anchor [1990s]
watch the eyelid movies [1960s+] (*eyelid movies* = sexual fantasies)

166

TO TAKE . . .

a beating [1960s+]
a load off one's mind [1990s]
a shake break [1990s]
an outing with Tom thumb and his four brothers [20C]
matters into one's own hands [20C]
one off the wrist [1960s+]
one's snake for a gallop [20C]
oneself in hand [1950s+]
the monster for a one-armed ride [1990s]

wave the magic wand [1990s]
wax the surfboard [20C]
whittle the stick [20C]
whiz jizzum [20C]
work off/oneself off [16C+]
wrestle the bald-headed champion [1990s]
yang one's wang [20C]
yank off [20C]
yank one's crank [20C] (US)
yank one's wank [20C]
yank the plank [1990s]
yankee one's wankee [20C]
yuck your choad [1960s+] (*yuck* = vomit, *choad* = penis)

'HITTING' THE PENIS

bash the candle [1990s]
bash the stick [1950s+] (Aus.)
battle the purple-helmeted warrior [1980s+]
belt it [1970s]
belt one's batter [1900s-40s]
biff off [1990s]
blast a pocket rocket [1990s]
boff [1930s+] (orig. US)
boff one's boner [1990s]
bomb the German helmet [1990s]
bop one's richard [1990s]
bounce one's boner [1990s]
box the bald champ [1990s]
box the bozack [1990s]
box the clown [1990s]

To Flog . . .

one's dong [20C]
one's donkey [late 19C+]
one's dumber brother [20C]
one's dummy [1970s+]
one's mutton [late 19C+]
the bishop [late 19C+]
the daisy [1950s+]
the dog [20C]
the dolphin/finless dolphin [1920s+]
the hog [20C]
the infidel [20C]
the log [1950s+]

And To Beat . . .

off [1960s+] (US)
one's dummy [1970s+]
one's hog [1970s+]
one's little brother [1960s+]
one's meat [late 19C+] (orig. US)
pete [1980s+]
the bald-headed bandit [1960s+]
the bishop [1960s+] (orig. US)
the bologna [20C]
the butter [1990s]
the dog [1930s+]
the pup [1950s] (US)
the stick [1990s]

box with richard [1990s] (i.e. 'dick')
buff one's helmet [1980s+]
buff the happy lamp [1980s+]
buff the wood [1990s]
bugger one's hand [1990s]
bludgeon the beefsteak [1980s+]
choke Kojak [1990s]
crack off/off a batch [1990s]
cuff one's dummy [1970s+]
flick the dick [1990s]
flip oneself off [1930s+] (Aus.)
flub the dub [20C] (US)
go a couple rounds with the ol' josh/champ [20C]
kill some babies [20C] (US)
mangle the midget [1990s]
plunk one's twanger [1990s]
pummel the love truncheon [1990s]
punch the clown [1990s]
punish percy in the palm [1990s]
rough up the suspect [1990s]
slam the hammer/wapper [1990s]
slog the log [1970s+]
snap the whip [1990s]
spank [1980s+] (US teen)
thump one's pumper [20C]
twang one's/the wire [1950s+]
twist one's crank [20C]
whack [1960s+]
whack/wack it [1960s+]
whack/wack willy [20C]
wonk one's conker [20C]

MILITARY

clean one's rifle [20C]
cock one's shotgun [1990s]
empty the cannon [1980s+]
fire the flesh musket [20C]
fire the hand cannon [20C]
fire the wobbly warhead [1980s+]
friendly fire [1980s+] (i.e. shots fired
    by one's own side)
load the cannon [1980s+]
man the cannon [1980s+]
man the cockpit [1980s+]
mount a corporal and four [late 18C-early 19C]
unload the gun [1990s]

...WAIT FOR IT!

TO WHIP . . .

it [20C]
off [20C] (US campus)
one's dripper [1990s]
one's dummy [1970s+]
one's lizard [1970s+]
one's wire [1970s+] (US campus)
the baloney pony [1990s]
the dummy [1990s]
the pony [1990s]
the weasel [1990s]
up some sour cream [1990s]

TO POUND . . .

off [1980s+] (US gay)
one's flounder [1990s]
one's meat [1950s+]
one's peenie [1960s]
one's pork [1960s]
one's pud [1960s]
the bald-headed moose [1990s]
the pelican [1990s]

OPERATING MACHINERY

adjust one's set [1980s+]
apply the hand brake [1980s+]
check one's oil [1930s+] (US)
clamp the pipe [1990s]
crimp the wire [1990s]
download one's floppy [1990s]
grease one's pipe [20C]
oil the glove [1990s]
prime one's pump [1950s+]
shift gears [1990s]
siphon/syphon off the tank [1990s]
stoke the furnace [1990s]
test one's batteries [1990s]

ANTI-CLERICAL

bash the priest [1990s]
batter the bishop [1990s]
box the Jesuit and get cockroaches
    [late 16C-early 19C]
buff the bishop [1980s+]
capture the bishop [1990s]
conk the cardinal [late 19C+]
disobey the pope [1980s+]
flip the bishop [late 19C+]
murder the bishop [late 19C+]
please the pope [1990s]
pummel the priest [1990s]
punish the pope [1990s]
rope the pope [1990s]

HOUSEWORK

defrost the fridge [1990s]
dust the end-table [1990s]
dust the family jewels [1990s]
iron some wrinkles [1990s]
organize the family jewels [1990s]
paint the ceiling [1990s]
sand the banister/wood [1990s]
unclog the drain/pipes [20C]
wax the buick [20C]
wax the car [20C]

NATURE STUDY

belt one's hog [20C] (US)
bleed the lizard [1990s]
burp the worm [1990s]
charm the serpent/snake [1990s]
choke the chicken/chook [20C]
choke the gopher [1970s+] (US)
come one's mutton [late 19C+]
come one's turkey [late 19C+]
corral the tadpoles [1990s]
crank the monkey [1990s]
cream one's beef [1990s]
cream one's cock [1990s]
cuff the dragon [1990s]
decongest the weasel [1990s]
drain the monster [1980s+]
feed the ducks [1990s] (US)
fight one's turkey [20C]
fish for zipper trout [1990s]
free willy [1990s] (play on the movie title)
gallop the old lizard [20C]
grapple the gorilla [1980s+]
hack the hog [20C]
hug the hog [1990s]
launch the tadpoles [1990s]
lift the lizard [1990s]
log the dog/hog [1990s]
lope the mule/the pony [1930s+] (US)
mess with moby [1990s] (i.e 'Moby Dick')
milk the chicken/chook [20C]

milk the lizard [late 19C+]
milk the maggot [late 19C+]
milk the moose [late 19C+]
molest the mole [1980s+]
pet the lizard [1970s+]
pluck one's chicken [1990s]
puff the one-eyed dragon [1960s+]
pump the monkey [1990s]
pump the python [1990s]
quiet the trouser snake [1990s]
ride the bull [1990s]
ride the dolphin [1920s+]
rope the goat/pony [1990s]
shemp the hog [1990s]
shoot tadpoles/the tadpoles [20C]
skin the goose [1970s] (US)
slay the one-eyed monster [1980s+]
snake [1980s+]
sperm the worm [1990s]
strangle the goose [1990s]
stroke one's lizard
stroke the dolphin/finless dolphin [1920s+]
swing the dolphin/finless dolphin [1920s+]
tame the beef weasel [1990s]
teach one's dog to spit [1990s]
tease one's crabs [1990s]
tease the weasel [1990s]
torment the trouser trout [1990s]
torture the tentacle [1990s]
tug one's slug [1990s]
walk the dog [20C]

wax the dolphin [20C]
whack/wack the one-eyed worm [1960s+]
whack/wack the weasel [1960s+]

CULINARY

accost the Oscar Meyer [1980s+] (i.e. the Oscar Meyer
    wiener)
adjust the bowl of fruit [1980s+]
beef-stroke-it-off [1990s] (play on 'beef stroganoff')
bob one's baloney [1990s]
bop one's baloney [1970s+]
buff the banana [1980s+]

175

bust a nut [1990s]
butter one's corn [20C]
butter the muffin [1990s]
cheese off [1990s]
churn butter [20C]
churn man cream [20C]
clear the custard [1990s]
cream one's corn [1990s]
cream the cheese [1990s]
cream the pie [1990s]
cuddle the kielbasa [1990s] (i.e. a kielbasa salami)
cuff the carrot [1990s]
frost the pastries [1990s]
hold the mayo [1990s]
hold the sausage hostage [1990s]
hone the cone [1990s]
kebab one's fist [1990s]
knead one's dough [1990s]
knead one's knockwurst [1990s]
knuckle the bone [1990s]
manipulate the mango [1990s]
massage the frankfurter [1950s] (Aus.)
master bacon [1990s]
milk [late 19C+]
milk one's dick [20C]
milk one's doodle [late 19C+]
milk oneself [late 19C+]
oscillate the Oscar Meyer [1990s] (US)
paddle the pickle [1990s]
paint the pickle [1990s]
peel some chillis [1990s]

peel the banana [1990s]
peel the carrot [1990s]
pip the pumpkin [1990s]
pop a nut [1960s+]
pump cream [1990s]
pump one's pickle [20C]
ram the ham [1990s]
roll the dough [1990s]
sample the secret sauce [1990s]
shake the bottle [1990s]
shell the bean pod [1990s]
shine the salami [1990s]

TO MASTURBATE IN RHYMING SLANG

rhyming with *wank*
bang the plank [1990s]
have a ham shank [20C]
have a Sherman [1980s+] (i.e. Sherman tank)
J. Arthur [1940s+] (i.e. J. Arthur Rank)
Levy And Frank [20C]
pull rank [20C]
Shabba [1990s] (i.e. from the reggae star Shabba Ranks)
shank [20C]
taxi-rank [1970s]
rhyming with *strop*
whip and top [20C]
rhyming with *toss*
polish and gloss [20C]

177

shuck the corn [20C]
slake the bacon [1990s]
slam the ham/salami/salmon [1950s+]
slam the spam [1990s]
slap the salami [1990s]
sling one's juice [19C]
squeeze the cheese [1990s]
stir one's stew/the batter [1950s+]
tease the weenie/wienie [1990s] (US)
toss the ham javelin [1990s]
tug one's taffy [1990s] (US)
tweak one's twinkie [20C]
wash the meat [20C]
yank the yam [20C]

TO MASTURBATE: THE WOMAN

apply lip gloss [1980s+]
baste the tuna [1980s+]
beat the beaver [1970s+]
brush the beaver [1990s]
bury the knuckle [1990s]
catch a buzz [1970s+] (i.e. masturbate with a vibrator)
clap one's clit [1970s+]
clean one's fur coat [1990s]
clout one's cookie [1970s] (US)
club the clam [1960s+]
cook cucumbers [1960s+] (i.e. use the cucumber as a dildo)
digitate [19C]
do something for my chapped lips [1980s+]
do the two-finger slot rumba [1990s]
do the two-fingered shuffle [1990s]
drill for oil [1940s] (orig. US Black)
finger fuck [1960s+]
finger pie [1950s+]
flick the bean [1990s]
floss the cat [1990s]
fondle the fig [1990s]
glaze the donut [1990s]
grease the gash [20C]
hit the slit [20C]
hose one's hole [20C] (i.e. use the stimulating qualities of a
    shower head)
hula-hoop [1990s]
itch the ditch [1990s]
lick one's lips [1990s]

179

light the candle [1990s]
lube the tube [1990s]
make waves/make waves for the man in the boat
    [1990s]
part the red sea [1990s]
perm one's poodle [1990s]
pet one's pussycat [1980s+]
pet the poodle [1960s+]
play stinky pinky [20C]
play the beaver [1990s]
play with the little man in the boat [20C]
poke one's pussy [1960s+]
poke the pucker [1990s]
preheat the oven [1990s]
ride the waterslide [1990s]
scratch the itch/patch [1990s]
slam the clam [1960s+]
sling one's jelly [19C]
stir it up [1950s+]
stump-jump [20C]
take a dip [1990s]
thumb [20C] (Irish)
tickle one's crack [19C]
wax the candle-stick [20C]
wax the womb [20C]
waz/wazz [1970s+] (lit. 'to urinate')
work in the garden [1990s]

Sex for Two

FOREPLAY

canoodle [mid-19C+] (US)
caterwaul [late 16C-late 19C]
fiddle [early 17C]
finkydiddle [late 19C-1940s]
firkytoodle [17C]
fumble [16C+]
grope [14C+]
guzzle [1930s]
make out [1940s+] (US)
mess [late 19C+]
nug [late 17C-19C]
peck and neck [1970s] (US Black)
warm up [1970s+]

STIMULATING THE VAGINA

clitorize [20C]
dildo [mid-17C-mid-19C]
feel one's way to heaven [19C]
finger [early 19C+]
finger fuck [late 18C+]
get a handful of sprats [late 19C+] (from the 'fishiness'
     of the vagina)
ling grapple [19C]
play stinkfinger [late 19C+]
tip the litle finger [19C]
tip the long finger [19C]
tip the middle finger [19C]

SEXUAL INTERCOURSE

bit of how's-yer-father [1940s+]
bit of the other [1920s+]
bonk [1970s+]
bunk-up [1930s+]
bush patrol [1950s+] (US)
the business [17C-18C]
dead shot [1970s+] (US Black)
four legged frolic [mid-19C]
fratting [1940s+]
the fruit that made man wise [17C]

●●

HORIZONTAL . . .

183

horizontal [1920s+] (US)
horizontal bop [1980s+] (US)
horizontal jogging [1970s+]
horizontal dancing [1950s+]
horizontal barn-dancing [1950s+]
horizontal mambo [1950s+]
horizontal polka [1950s+]
horizontal polo [1950s+]
horizontal refreshment [late 19C+]
horizontal relaxation [1940s+] (Aus./N.Z.)
horizontal rhumba [1950s+]
horizontal rumble [1950s+]
horizontals [1920s-30s] (US)
horizontal twist and shout [1960s]

●●

ginicomtwig [late 16C-early 17C]
ground rations [1930s-40s] (US Black)
horry [1940s+] (Aus./N.Z.; abbr. 'horizontal')
hot fling [20C]
houghmagandy [20C] (Ulster/Scot.; adulterous sex)
indoor sledging [20C]
interior decorating [1980s+]
jack in the box [1970s+] (US Black)
lap clap [17C]
lay [mid-17C; 1920s+]
legover [1940s+]
matrimonial [19C] (i.e. sex in the missionary position)
nasty [1960s-70s]
naughties [1950s+]

nobbing [20C]
nookie [1920s+] (orig. US)
oats [1920s+]
parallel parking [1980s+] (US campus/teen)
roll in the hay [1920s+]
rubadub [1950s] (US)
shift service [19C]

SPONTANEOUS INTERCOURSE

bip-bam-thank-you ma'am [20C]
bump [1970s+]
fast-fuck [20C]
quickie [1940s+]
wham bam thank-you ma'am [late 19C+]

shift work [19C]
sport of Venus [19C]
straight shot [1970s+] (US Black)
thrill and chill [1970s+] (US Black)
turking [20C]
Ugandan discussions [1970s+] (from the discovery
    in flagrante of a Ugandan politician in an airport
    lavatory)
you know what [20C]

SEXUAL INTERCOURSE: SPECIALITIES

afternoon delight [1960s+] (sex in the afternoon)
bagpiping [late 19C] (*coitus in axilla*, i.e. intercourse
    under the armpit)
dog's match [19C+] (sex in the bushes)
dry bob [late 17C-18C] (sex without ejaculation)
flash in the pan [1980s+] (sex without ejaculation)
funch [20C] (i.e. 'fucking after lunch')
knee-trembler [late 19C+] (sex standing up)
melting moments [19C] (two fat people having sex)
nooner [1970s+] (adulterous lunchtime sex)
perpendicular [mid-late 19C] (sex standing up)
pre-dawn vertical insertion [1980s] (sex in the early
    morning, from a description by President Reagan of
    the 1983 US invasion of Grenada)
roofing it [1950s+] (US; having sex on the roof)
sportfuck [1960s+] (spontaneous casual sex)
talking fuck [1960s+] ('talking dirty')

HAVING SEXUAL INTERCOURSE

BANGING, DRILLING AND POUNDING

bang [late 17C+]
beat with an ugly stick [1980s+] (US campus)
bonk [1970s+]
bop [1970s] (US)
bore [18C]
bounce [19C+]
bounce refrigerators [1980s+] (US campus)
bump bellies [20C] (US)
bump fuzz [1980s+] (US campus)
bump uglies [1970s+] (US Black/teen)
bushwhack [1910s-40s] (US campus)
bust/beat one's nuts [1940s+]
carve a slice [20C]
do a grind [mid-19C+]
drill [18C+]
drill for oil [1940s] (orig. US Black)
flimp [mid-late 19C] (Flemish *flimpe*, 'to hit in the face')
give a tumble [20C]
grind [mid-17C+]
grind one's coffee [1920s] (US)
hammer a job [1940s+] (Irish)
hit [1940s+] (US)
hit skins [20C]
hump [late 18C+]
hustle [19C]
impale [19C]
jab [1980s+] (US campus)

jolt [19C]

jounce [19C] (lit. 'to shake')

juke [1940s+] (orig. W.I./US Black; lit. 'to stab')

jump on someone's bones [mid-19C+]

knock [late 16C+]

knock boots [1980s+] (US Black/campus)

knock off [1930s+] (orig. US)

krunk [1990s] (i.e. 'crunch')

labour leather [18C+]

lash [1950s] (W.I.)

lay [mid-17C-mid-18C; 19C+]

make [1910s+] (US)

make her grunt [20C]

make her scream [1980s+] (US campus)

mollock [1930s+] (dial. *marlock*, to play)

nodge [17C]

nub [late 17C-early 19C]

peg [mid-19C]

perforate [late 19C+]

pile [1970s+] (US Black/campus)

plank [1960s+]

plonk [20C]

plough/plow [1950s+] (US)

plough/plow the back forty [1950s+] (US)

plowter [19C] (dial. 'to splash about in mud')

pluck [1960s+] (US Black)

plug [late 18C+] (lit. 'to fill in')

poke [mid-19C+]

pot the white [1930s+]

pound [1970s+] (US Black)

prang [1940s+] (lit. 'to crash')

prig [late 17C-18C] (i.e. 'to prick')
prod [late 19C+]
pump [18C+]
rage [1970s+] (Aus./N.Z./US campus)
ram [late 19C+]
rasp [late 19C-1900s]
ride [late 18C+]
ride below the crupper [19C]
rip off [1950s+] (US Black)
rock [20C] (orig. US Black)
rock and roll [1990s]
rock one's world [1980s+] (US campus)
romp [1980s+] (US campus)
root [1950s+] (Aus.)
rort [1940s+] (Aus./N.Z.)
roust [late 16C-early 17C]
rumbusticate [late 19C-1900s]
rummage [19C]
schtup [1950s+] (German *stupsen*, to push)
scrag [1930s+] (US)

To Bury . . .

it [mid-19C+]
old Fagin [1950s]
one's bone [1980s+] (US Black teen)
the baldy fella/fellow [1980s+] (Irish)
the fang [1950s+]
the tomahawk [20C] (US)

scrape [1950s+] (Aus.)
screw [early 18C+]
scrouperize [mid-17C-early 18C] (lit. 'to rub against')
shag [late 18C+] (lit. 'to shake')
shake [16C-1900s]
shake a skin-coat [16C]
shake a tart [late 19C+]
shake the sheets [18C]
shoot [late 19C+]
shoot between/betwixt wind and water
    [late 17C-1900s]
shoot in the bush [1950s+]
shoot in the stubble [18C-19C]
shoot in the tail [mid-19C+]
sink the little man in the boat [20C]
sink the soldier [20C]
skeeze [1980s+] (US Black; dial. *skeese*, to frisk about)
slam [1980s+] (US Black/campus/W.I./UK Black teen)
slap skins [1990s] (orig. US Black)
snabble [19C+] (dial. 'to eat greedily')
sned [20C] (Ulster; lit. 'to cut off')
snizzle [1910s-20s] (dial. 'to wriggle')
sock it to [1960s] (orig. US Black)
spear the bearded clam [1960s+] (Aus.)
spear the hairy doughnut [1990s]
spit [late 18C-late 19C]
split [late 18C+]
spread [mid-19C]
stab [late 16C-early 17C]
stab in the main vein [1950s+]
stab in the thigh [19C]

189

stick [19C+]
strike [mid-16C-mid-18C]
stuff [1950s+]
swinge [17C] (lit. 'to beat')
throw a fuck/boff/bop/screw into [20C] (US)
throw a leg over [early 18C+]
throw the D [1980s+] (US Black; i.e. the 'dick')
throw the dagger [1980s+] (US campus)
throw the harpoon in/into [1960s] (US)
throw ass/some ass [1950s+] (US Black)
thrum [late 17C-early 19C] (lit. 'to play a stringed
    instrument')

190

TO DANCE . . .

on the mattress [19C]
Sallinger's round [17C-early 18C]
the blanket hornpipe [19C]
the buttock jig [19C]
the goat's jig [19C]
the kipples [19C]
the married man's cotillion [19C]
the matrimonial polka [19C]
the mattress jig [19C]
the miller's reel [19C]
the reels o' Bogie [18C-19C] (Scot.)
the reels of Stumpie [18C-19C] (Scot.)
to the tune of shaking the sheets
    (without music) [19C]
with your arse to the ceiling [19C]

tonk [1910s+] (Aus.)
towze [early 17C-mid-18C]
tumble [early 17C+]
thump [1980s+] (US teen)
wax [1980s+]
wax some ass [1970s+] (US Black)
whop it up [1960s+]
womp/whomp on [1980s+] (US campus)
work [20C] (orig. US Black)
work one's bot [20C]

USING THE GENITALS

ball slap [1990s]
cock [19C+]
dick [20C] (mainly US Black)
dibble [19C]
diddle [mid-19C+] (orig. US)
doodle [late 19C+]
dork [1960s+] (orig. US)
get one's hole [1960s+]
join paunches [18C]
knob [20C]
lance [1960s] (US)
lay some pipe [1930s+] (US)
make a settlement in tail [late 17C-early 18C] (play on the
    legal term 'entail')
nail two wames together [18C] (Scot. *wame*, the belly)
peel one's best end in [late 19C-1910s]
park the pink cadillac [1990s]
pestle [late 19C-1900s]

pizzle [18C-19C] (lit. a 'bull's penis')
pole [19C+]
pop it in [late 19C+]
prick [late 16C+]
prong [1940s+] (US Black)
put barney in the VCR (US Black)
quiff [early 18C-19C]
quim [early 18C+]
rod [late 19C+]
shaft [1950s+] (orig. US)
skin the cat [19C+]
skin the pizzle [mid-19C-1900s]
slip her a length [1940s+]
slip her a quick crippler [1940s+]
slip in Daintie Davie [19C] (Scot.)
slip in Willie Wallace [19C] (Scot.)
slip it to her [1940s+]
spike [20C]
squeeze the lemon [1930s+] (orig. US Black)
stiff [1930s+]
stretch leather [18C+]
strop one's beak [19C]
tail [late 18C+]
tool [mid-18C-late 19C]
varnish the cane [late 19C-1960s] (US)

ANIMAL SEX

buck [mid-16C+]
bull [18C+]
catch fleas for someone [19C-1910s]

chuck a tread [late 19C-1900s] (usu. of cocks and hens)
clicket [17C-early 19C] (usu. of foxes)
dog [late 19C+]
exercise the ferret [1960s+]
ferret [19C]
grease the weasel [1990s] (US teen)
hog [19C]
horse [17C; 1950s+]
lead the llama to the lift shaft [1990s]
play the goat [18C]
put on dog [mid-19C+] (US)
ride the hobby horse [1980s+] (US campus)
roger [early 18C+] (*roger* = bull)
sling fish [1980s+] (US)
stick one's duck in the mud [1970s] (US)
tether one's nags on [19C] (Scot. lit. 'tie up one's horse')
tom [19C] (Scot.)
tread [16C] (usu. of cocks and hens)
tup [late 16C+] (usu. of goats)

193

SEXUAL INTERCOURSE IN RHYMING SLANG

rhyming with *fuck*
    Donald Duck [1960s+] (Aus.)
    friar tuck [late 19C+]
    goose and duck [late 19C+]
    trolley/trolley and truck [1910s+]
rhyming with *arse*
    bottle (and glass) [20C]

'MEATY' SEX

be in a woman's beef [late 18C-mid-19C]
bury the brisket [1950s+] (US)
cut a side [late 18C+]
cut a slice off the joint [late 18C+]
give someone some meat [1950s+]
have a bit of giblet pie [19C]
have a bit of meat [late 19C+]
have a bit of mutton [mid-16C+]
have a bit of pork [18C+]
have a bit of split mutton [18C-1900s]
have a bit off the chump end [20C]
have a jumble giblets [17C]
have/do a bit of beef [late 19C+]
hide one's/the baloney [1920s] (US)
hide the sausage [1940s] (Aus.)
hide the weenie/wienie [1910s] (US)
join giblets [18C]
mash the fat [1970s+] (US Black)
mix giblets [18C]
pork [1970s+]
pour the pork [1950s+] (orig. US)
pull the bacon [1990s]
put four quarters on the spit [18C]
put the meat to [20C]
rub offal [1990s]
sink the sausage [1980s+]
stir the stew [1900s-10s]
stretch some meat [1980s+] (US)

TO GET . . .

a crumpet [1930s+]
a piece [1980s+]
a shot of crack [20C] (US)
a shot of leg [1970s+] (US Black)
an encore [20C] (i.e. a second bout of intercourse)
busy [1990s] (US Black/teen)
get some tail [1970s+] (US)
gravel for one's goose [1930s+] (US)
horizontal [1970s+] (orig. US)
into someone's pants [1960s+]
it wet [20C]
on the old fork [late 19C-1900s]
on top of [1980s+]
one's agates cracked [1940s+] (US)
one's axle greased [1960s]
one's banana peeled [late 19C+] (orig. US)
one's batteries charged [1930s+] (US)
one's cookies [1950s+]
one's corn ground [early 19C] (US)
one's dipper wet [1980s+] (US)
one's end in [1930s+]
one's jollies [1950s+]
one's lance waxed [1980s]
one's leg dressed [18C]
one's oats [1920s+]
one's rocks off [1940s+]
one's swerve on [1970s] (US Black)
shot in the tail [late 17C-early 18C]
some skins [1990s] (US Black)

sloppy [1980s] (US Black/campus)
some big leg [1970s+] (US Black)
some cock [20C] (US Black/South; *cock* = vagina)
some pink [1990s] (US)
some pussy [1970s+] (US)
some tail [1970s+] (US)
the drawers [20C] (US Black)

TO GIVE . . .

a bit of legover [1940s+]
a bit of hard for soft [late 19C]
her a length [1940s+]
her a tail [1960s+]
her one [late 19C+]
some body [1960s+]
someone a jump [20C]
someone a shot [19C+]
someone a tumble [20C]
someone one [late 19C+]
someone the business [1940s+] (orig. US)
the boots to [1930s+]
the dog a bone [1980s+]
the lizard a run [1960s+] (Aus.)

TO GO . . .

all the way/the whole way [1920s+]
ballocking [19C+]
bang [1920s+] (Aus.)
beard-splitting [18C]

bed-pressing [19C]
belly-bumping [19C]
birds-nesting [20C]
bitching [late 17C-mid-19C]
bottom hole working [20C]
bum fighting [early-mid-18C]
bum-faking [early-mid-18C]
bum-tickling [early-mid-18C]
bum-working [early-mid-18C]
bush ranging [20C]
buttock-stirring [late 18C-early 19C]
buttocking [18C]
cockfighting [19C]
cunny-catching [18C]
drabbing [early 16C-19C] (*drab* = wench)
fleshing it [mid-late 19C]
fleshmongering [17C]
goosing [mid-19C+]
hunting [20C]
jumming [17C] (dial. *jum*, a sudden jolt)
leather-stretching [late 16C-18C]
molrowing [mid-late 19C] (lit. 'making a woman scream')
motting [19C] (lit. 'womanising')
pile driving [20C]
prick scouring [17C-19C]
quim wedging [19C]
quim-sticking/wedging [19C]
rump splitting [19C]
rumping [19C+]
sticking [19C]
strumming [19C]

tail tickling/twitching [late 17C-early 18C]
to Hairyfordshire [19C]
tromboning [20C]
tummy tickling [mid-late 19C]
twat faking/raking [1900s-20s]
twatting [1900s-20s]
under petticoating [19C]
up her petticoats [19C]
vaulting [late 16C-late 17C]
wenching [early 17C-early 18C]
working the dumb/hairy oracle [late 18C-mid-19C]

TO HAVE OR DO A BIT OF . . .

business [mid-19C+]
cauliflower [18C; 1990s]
cock [20C]
cock-fighting [19C]
cream stick [19C]
cunt [late 17C+]
curly greens [late 19C+]
dancing [mid-late 19C]
fish on a fork [mid-19C-1900s]
jam [1960s+]
ladies' tailoring [mid-19C-1920s]
quimsy [19C]
rough [mid-19C+]
sharp and blunt [20C] (rhy. sl. 'cunt')
skirt [20C]
stuff [late 19C+]
summer cabbage [19C]

TO HAVE OR DO OR PERFORM A/THE . . .

back scuttle [19C]
ballocking [19C+]
banana [1910s+]
beanfeast in bed [late 19C+]
bedward bit [19C]
belly warmer [19C]
bit of rabbit-pie [19C]
bit of stuff [late 19C+]
blindfold bit [19C]
blow-through [late 19C+]
bone dance [1980s+] (US campus)
bottom wetter [late 19C+]
brush with the cue [19C]
a cut/a slice off the joint [late 18C+]
dash in the bloomers [1960s+]
dash up the Channel [20C]
dingo [1990s]
dirties/dirty deed [1960s+] (orig. US teen/campus)
dive in the dark [18C-late 19C]
dog's marriage/match [19C+]
four legged frolic [mid-19C]
game in the cock loft [mid-17C-18C]
goose and duck [late 19C+] (rhy. sl. 'fuck')
grind [mid-17C+]
little of one with the other [19C]
plaster of warm guts [late 18C-early 19C]
poke [mid-19C+]
roger [early 18C+]
roll/roll in the hay [1920s+]

rootle [mid-19C-1920s]
shag [late 18C+]
shoot up the straight [mid-late 19C]
shot at the bull's eye [late 17C]
slide up the board [late 19C]
squirt and a squeeze [mid-19C]
tumble in a wet 'un [20C]
wipe at the place [mid-late 19C]

TO PLAY AT . . .

Adam and Eve [19C]
all fours [19C]
belly-to-belly [19C]
brangle [early-mid-17C] (lit. 'shake')
buttock [early 18C]
buttock and leave her [late 17C-mid-18C]
cherry pit [20C]
cock in cover [19C]
couple your navels [18C]
couple/cuddle my cuddie [19C]
fathers and mothers [1940s+]
Handie Dandie [16C] (Scot.)
Hey Gammer Cook [18C]
Hooper's Hide [20C] (i.e. 'hide-and-seek')
in and in [17C]
in and out [19C]
Irish whist [20C]
itch-buttocks [late 16C-19C]
lift-leg [early 18C-mid-19C]
mumble-peg [late 19C]

prick the garter [mid-19C]
push-pin/push-pike [17C-18C]
rantum-scantum [late 18C-early 19C]
stable my naggie [18C-19C]
the first game ever played [19C]
the organ [20C] (Aus.)
thread the needle [1930s+]
tiddlywinks [20C]
tops and bottoms [20C]
two handed put [18C-early 19C] (a pun on Eng. *put (in)*
    + French *putain*, a whore)
up tails all [late 17C-early 18C]
where the Jack takes Ace [19C]
wriggle your navels [18C]

TO TAKE A TURN . . .

among her frills [19C]
among the cabbages [19C]
among the parsley [19C]
in Bushey Park [19C]
in Cock Lane [19C]
in Cupid's Alley [19C]
in Cupid's Corner [19C]
in Hair Court [19C]
in Cock Alley [19C]
in Love Lane [19C]
on Mount Pleasant [19C]
on Shooter's Hill [1970s] (US Black)
through the stubble [18C-19C]
up her petticoats [19C]

THE EARLIEST TERMS

sard [10C-17C] (appears in the 10C *Lindisfarne Gospel*)
foin [14C] (lit. 'to thrust with a pointed weapon')
swive [mid-15C+]

A 16TH-CENTURY SELECTION

feeze/pheeze
flesh/flesh it
ginicomtwig
grope for trout in a peculiar river (from
    William Shakespeare's *Measure for Measure*)
jumble
make the beast with two backs (from William
    Shakespeare's *Othello*)
tonygle (i.e. 'to niggle')

A 17TH-CENTURY SELECTION

blow off the loose corns
blow the groundsels
bumfiddle
go on Hobbes' voyage (the last words of the writer
    Thomas Hobbes spoke of 'a great leap in the dark')
jumm (lit. 'to jolt')
jump up and down
lerricompoop
play at pickle-me-tickle-me
poop
twang

AN 18TH-CENTURY SELECTION

Adam and Eve it
engage in/play at three to one (and bound to lose)
do it
get one's leg across/over/dressed
go facemaking (refers to the face of the new baby that
    may result)
huddle
lift a leg on/over
palliardise
shoot London Bridge
wind up the clock

A 19TH-CENTURY SELECTION

Adamize
be after one's greens
bellybump
dip it
dip one's wick
dip the fly
dive into the dark
do a bit of front-door work
feed the dumb glutton
feed the dummy
frig
frisk
get jack in the orchard
get one's end away
get one's greens

give someone a seeing-to
have a bit of bum
jiggy-jig
nibble
oblige
paddle
perform on
put the devil into hell
rump
see the stars lying on one's back (of a woman)
strain one's greens
wallop it in
whack it up

204

THE 'F' WORD: A SHORT HISTORY

foutra/foutre [16C] (French)
fuck [late 17C+] (origin uncertain; one theory is that it
    comes from Latin *pugnare*, 'to fight or strike')
fugle [early 18C-late 19C]
fulke [early 19C] (euphemism coined by Lord Byron)
fucky-fucky [late 19C+]
futter [late 19C+] (from French *foutre*)
fickey-fick [20C]
fuckle [20C]
fug [1940s+] (euphemism coined by Norman Mailer)
futz [1940s+]
fugh [1950s+] (euphemism coined by Brendan Behan)

A 20TH-CENTURY SELECTION

ball
dip the schnitzel
do the nasty
do the natural thing
do the pussy
drop one's load
empty one's trash
lay the leg
lift arse on
love up
make it with
meddle with
mess around
nail
play hide the salami
play it on the throat
play mummies and daddies
play night baseball
polish one's arse on the top sheet
reel in the biscuit
score
score between the posts
score ten
wind one's ball of yarn

YEAHSSS!

205

THE MALE ANGLE

action [1920s+] (orig. US Black)
all there but the most of you [mid-19C-1940s]
balling [1930s+] (orig. US Black)
booting [1920s-30s] (US Black)
bottom hole working [20C]
caught with rem-in-re [mid-19C] (lit. 'thing in thing')

To Have Enthusiastic Intercourse

bang like a hammer on a nail [1950s+] (orig. Aus.)
bang like a rattlesnake [1950s+] (orig. Aus.)
bang like the dunny/shithouse door in a gale
    [1960s+] (Aus.)
fuck like a bunny [20C] (of a woman)
fuck like a mink [1910s+] (Aus.)
fuck like a stoat [late 19C]
fuck the arse/ass off [1960s+]
go as if she cracked nuts with her tail [late 17C-
    early 18C]
go for it [1920s+]
go in and out like a fiddler's elbow [20C]
go like a train [20C]
go up like a rat up a drain [1960s+] (orig. Aus.)
be nimble hipped [19C]
rip her guts down [1970s+] (US Black)
screw the arse off [1950s+]
shag like a rattlesnake [1960s+]

dunking [1900s]
federating [1900s-10s] (Aus.; puns on *federate* = join
    together)
gaying it [18C]
in her mutton [19C]
in the saddle [20C]
in the skins [1990s] (US Black)
jazzing [1950s] (US)
on the box [20C] (Irish)
on the grind [late 19C+]
on the job [19C+]
packing [1990s] (US Black)
prick-chinking [18C]
prigging [late 16C-18C]
tomming [1930s+]
up her way [late 19C+]
up to no good [1980s+]
up to your nuts-in-guts [1990s] (orig. Aus.)

THE FEMALE ANGLE

catch an oyster [19C]
do a back fall [19C]
do a spread [mid-19C]
do a tumble [1900s]
do a wet 'un [19C]
do the naughty [1950s+] (Aus./N.Z.)
do what Eve did with Adam
do what mother did before me [19C]
do a wet bottom [19C]
do/have/perform a bottom-wetter [19C]

draw off [19C]
drop 'em [20C]
drop one's tweeds [20C]
feed one's pussy [20C]
get a bellyful of marrow pudding [mid-19C]
get a bit of goose's neck [late 19C]
get a go at the creamstick [19C+]
get a green gown [16C-19C] (i.e. by having *al fresco* sex)
get a handle for the broom [19C]

COITUS INTERRUPTUS

get off/out at Broadgreen [20C] (the station before Edge Hill, near Liverpool)

get off/out at Edge Hill [20C] (the station before Liverpool Lime Street)

get off/out at Gateshead [20C] (the station before Newcastle)

get off/out at Haymarket [20C] (the station before Edinburgh Waverley)

get off/out at Hillgate [1970s+]

get off/out at Paisley [20C] (the station before Glasgow Central)

get off/out at Redfern [1970s+] (Aus.; the station before Sydney Central)

leave before the gospel [20C] (i.e. before the church service is fully over)

make a coffeehouse of a woman's cunt [late 18C]

swerve [1950s+] (Aus.)

get a wet bottom [19C]
get a shove in one's blind eye [late 18C-1900s]
get one's chimney swept (out) [19C]
get one's kettle mended [17C]
get one's leather stretched [18C+]
get one's leg lifted [early 18C-late 19C]
get outside/outside of [late 19C+]
get shot in the tail [late 17C-early 18C]
get some rod [1990s] (US campus)
get stabbed in the thigh [19C]
get what Harry gave Doll [18C-19C]
give a hot poultice for the Irish toothache
     (*Irish toothache* = an erection)
give juice for jelly [19C]
give mutton for beef [19C]
give soft for hard [19C]
give standing room for one only [19C]
go star-gazing/star-gazing on one's back
     [late 18C-mid-19C]
go to buck [early 18C]
have a bit of gut stick [1970s]
have a bit of sugar stick [19C]
have a live sausage for supper [19C]
have an itchy back [1920s+] (Aus.)
have hot pudding for supper [19C+]
lift one's leg [early 18C-late 19C]
light the lamp [late 19C-1920s]
look at the ceiling [20C]
lose the match and pocket the stakes [19C]
open up [mid-19C+]
play one's ace [1990s]

pray with one's knees upwards [late 18C-early 19C]
ride a St George [19C] (i.e. the woman is on top)
ride the baloney pony [1990s] (US)
see the stars lying upon one's back [19C]
skin the live rabbit [19C]
slip it about [20C]
spread for [mid-19C]
stand/do the push [late 19C+]
stare at the ceiling [20C]
suck the sugar-stick [19C]
take in and do for [mid-19C]
take in beef [mid-19C]
take in cream [late 19C+]
take one's medicine [mid-late 19C]
throw ass/some ass [1950s+] (US Black)
throw the P [1980s+] (US Black; P = 'pussy')
turn up [mid-late 17C]
turn up one's tail [late 17C-early 18C]
wind one's clock [1970s] (US)
wrap the sub [1990s] (US campus)

210

NATIONAL SEX STYLES

American culture [1960s+] ('straight' intercourse)
Chinese fashion [1960s+] (on one's side)
English culture [1960s+] (bondage and discipline)
Greek culture/love [1930s+] (anal sex)
Roman culture [1960s+] (orgies)
Swedish culture [1960s+] (rubber fetishism)

REAR ENTRY

doggy fashion [1960s+]
dog it [1940s+]
dog-style/doggy-style [1950s+]
dogways [late 19C]
go in by the servant's entrance [1960s+]

PLACES FOR SEX

babe lair [1980s+] (US)
body exchange [1960s-70s] (e.g. a singles bar)
body shop [1970s+] (US)
cafeteria [1980s+] (US gay)
cock wagon [1970s] (US)
cunt wagon [1970s+] (US)
fuck pad [1950s+] (orig. US)
fuck truck [1970s+] (Aus.)
hay [20C] (i.e. a bed)
killing floor [1970s+] (US Black)
love shack [1960s+] (orig. US)
meat market [1950s+]
pig room [1980s+] (US gay; a room for orgies)
saddling paddock [mid-late 19C] (Aus.)
shag-wagon [1960s+]
shagging-wagon [1960s+]
slaughterhouse [1970s] (US Black)
watering hole [1960s+] (gay; usu. a park or bar)
whip-shack [1970s+] (US Black)
zipper club [1980s+] (US gay; a location, such as a
    bath-house, for repeated oral sex)

211

THE ORGASM

big O [1950s+]
blast-off [1960s] (US)
come [mid-17C+]
cum [1920s+]
double-barrel [1990s] (more than one orgasm in a single
    session of sex)
double master-blaster [1980s] (an orgasm reached
    through fellatio and the simultaneous smoking of a pipe
    of crack cocaine)
final gallop [1990s]
flock/nest of sparrows flying out of one's backside
    [1950s+] (Aus.)
jolly [1960s+] (US)
load [1920s+] (US)
nut [1960s+] (US)
paradise strokes [20C] (i.e. the thrusts that immediately
    precede orgasm)
pop [mid-19C+]
short strokes [20C] (i.e. the thrusts that immediately
    precede orgasm)
spendings [mid-late 19C]
thrill [1910s+]

TO REACH ORGASM

blast off [1960s] (US)
blow [1970s+] (orig. US)
blow one's cork [1930s+] (US)
blow one's hump [1950s+] (US)

blow one's juice [1990s]
blow one's lot [1940s+] (Aus.)
bust [1960s] (US Black)
bust a nut [1990s]
bust/beat one's nut/nuts [1940s+] (US)
bust one's kicks off [1920s+] (US)
cock [1960s+] (US Black)
come [mid-17C+]
come off [17C+]
cum [1950s+]
get a nut [1990s]
get home [19C]
get it/'em/one off [1930s+] (US)
get off [1970s+] (orig. US Black)
get off the button [1930s] (US)
get one's jones off [1960s+] (orig. US Black)
get one's kicks off [1920s+] (US)
get one's rocks off [1940s+]
go [18C]
go off [1920s+]
go up the rainbow [1970s]
let go [late 19C+]
light off [late 19C+]
light up [1940s-50s]
make it [1950s+] (US)
make one's love come down [1950s-60s] (US Black)
melt [mid-19C+]
off [late 17C+]
plug in the neon [1960s+] (US gay; refers to the practice of
    inhaling amyl nitrate at the moment of orgasm)
pop one's cork [1960s+]

213

    pop one's nuts [1920s+] (orig. US)
    put/keep the anchors on [1970s+] (i.e. to delay orgasm)
    ready to spit [20C]
    spend [mid-17C-late 19C]

TO EJACULATE

    blow one's load [1990s]
    blow one's tubes [1990s]
    crack one's marbles [1930s] (US)
    crack one's nuts [1940s-60s] (US)
    double one's milt [19C] (i.e. to ejaculate twice without
        withdrawing)
    fetch [late 19C+]
    fire a shot [late 19C+]
    get one's balls off [1960s] (orig. US)
    get one's gun/gun off [1960s]
    get one's nuts off [1930s+] (orig. US Black)
    pop one's nuts [1920s+] (orig. US)
    ranch [1920s+] (US)
    shoot one's load [1920s+]
    shoot one's milt [mid 19C-1910s]
    shoot one's rocks [1940s+]
    shoot one's roe [mid 19C-1900s]
    shoot one's wad [1920s+] (orig. US)

TO GIVE SOMEONE AN ORGASM

bring on the china [1900s-30s]
bring someone off [20C]
bust someone out [1980s+] (US Black)
do her job for her [mid-19C+]
give one's gravy [19C]
give someone a thrill [1910s+]
make the chimney smoke [mid-19C+]
pop someone off [1950s+] (orig. US)
pop someone's cookies [1970s+]
pop someone's nuts [1950s+]
ring someone's bell [1910s+]
ring someone's chimes [1970s+] (orig. US)

THE CONDOM

bag [1920s+] (US)
baggie [1970s+] (US)
balloon [1950s+]
bishop [late 18C]
body bag [1990s]
boot [1970s+] (US)
cape [1980s+] (US)
Casanova's rubber
   sock [1990s]
cheater [1940s] (US)
Coney Island whitefish [1940s+] (US; from the used
   condoms that float in the sea off Coney Island)

cum drum [1960s+]
diving-suit [1940s+] (Aus.)
f.e. [1990s] (S.Afr.; 'French envelope')
flunky [20C]
flute mute [1990s]
franger [1970s+] (Aus.)
French cap [1920s] (US)
French letter [mid-19C+]
French safe [1910s+]
French tickler [1910s+]
frenchie [mid-19C+]
frikkie [1970s+] (S.Afr.; i.e. 'frig-gy')
frog [1950s+] (orig. Aus.; pun on 'French')
frogskin [1920s+] (orig. Aus./N.Z.)
fuck rubber [1980s]
glove [1950s+] (US)
hat [20C] (US)
head gasket [1960s+] (US)
helmet [1990s] (US Black teen)
jacket [1960s+] (US)
jimmy cap [1980s+] (US Black)
jimmy protector [1980s+] (US Black)

216

SEX WITH CONTRACEPTION

boot up [1970s+] (US Black)
fight in armour [late 18C]
have one's boots on [1980s+] (US Black)
in one's armour [late 18C]

SEX WITHOUT CONTRACEPTION

bareback [1950s+]
button lurk [1910s] (Aus.)
do the deadly deed [1980s+] (US campus)
not go to bed with one's boots on [1950s+]
raw [1990s] (US)
raw dogg [1990s] (US Black teen)
ride bareback [1950s+]
Roman roulette [1960s]
straight shot [1970s+] (US Black)
vatican roulette [1920s+]

jitbag [1990s]
jizzbag [1980s+]
jo-bag [1960s+]
john [1960s+]
johnnie [1960s+]
jolly bag [1980s+] (US)
lifejacket [1980s+] (US campus)
love envelope [1980s+]
love glove [1980s+] (US)
lube [1970s+] (US)
lubie [1970s+] (US)
machine [late 18C]
merry widow [1920s-30s] (US)
Mrs Philip's purse [late 18C] (as sold by a well-known madame)
one-piece overcoat [1950s+]

overcoat [1920s-70s]
party hat [1980s+] (orig. US campus)
phallic thimble [1920s-30s]
pro [1940s-50s] (US; abbr. of *prophylactic*)
raincoat [1950s+]
Reggie and Ronnie [1960s+] (rhy. sl. 'johnny')
rozzer [1970s] (US Black)
rubber [1940s+] (orig. US)
rubber boot [1970s+]
rubber johnny [1950s+]
scumbag [1920s+]
sheepskin [1990s] (US campus; an allegedly superior material for condoms)
skin [1990s] (US Black)
washer [1980s+] (US gay)
wise monkey [20C] (rhy. sl. 'flunky')

FEMALE CONTRACEPTIVES

b.c. [1960s-80s] (US Black; i.e. *birth control*)
catcher's mitt [1980s+] (US)
fuck-plug [1980s+]
mother's friend [19C]
pussy butterfly [1970s] (US; from the shape of an IUD)
roll [1970s+] (US Black)

218

Oral Sex

ORAL SEX IN GENERAL

face [1960s+] (US)
flying sixty-six [20C] (rhy. sl. 'French tricks')
French tricks [mid-19C-20C]
Frencher [20C]
head [1940s+]
header [1970s+] (US)
lip action [20C] (US)
lip dancing [20C] (US)
lip music [20C] (US)
lunch [1940s+]
plating [1960s+] (rhy. sl. 'plates of meat' = 'eat')
skull job [1950s+]
tongue job [1960s+] (orig. US)

TO PERFORM ORAL SEX

bag [1950s+] (US Black)
chow down [1950s+] (US)
eat [1920s+]
eat it [1910s+]
feed one's face [20C]
gamo/gammo [1910s+] (abbr. of *gamahuche*)
get down [1930s] (US)
give a perm [1980s+] (US campus)
go below 14th street [1960s]
go down [1910s+] (US)
go down for the gravy [1950s+]
goop [1960s+] (US; abbr. 'gobble the goop')
have lunch downtown [1920s+]

knock the dust off the old sombrero [20C] (US)
munch [1970s+]
orbit [1980s+] (one 'goes round' the genitals)
sit on someone's face [1960s+]
skull [1970s+] (orig. US Black; play on 'head')
slob a knob [1940s+] (US)
swing low [1990s] (US Black teen)

FELLATIO

army style [1960s+] (US gay; fellatio followed by the
    beating up of the fellator)
Barry Johnson [1990s] (i.e. 'blow job')
basket job [1950s+]
blow job/b.j. [1940s+] (orig. US)
cocksuck [1940s+] (orig. US)
cocksucking [20C] (orig. US)
deep throat [1970s+]
dicklick [1980s+] (US gay)
dicksucking [1970s+]
face pussy [1980s+] (US gay)
face-fucking [1970s+]
French [late 19C+]
French culture [1960s+]
French head job [1940s+]
French love [20C]
French style [20C]
French way [20C]
gam/gamb [20C] (abbr. of gamahuche)

221

gob job [1980s+] (US gay)
gobble [late 19C+]
gumjob [1980s+] (US)
hard mouthful [20C]
hat job [1950s+] (orig. US)
head job [1950s+] (orig. US)
hose job [1970s+] (US)
hum [1960s+] (US)
hum-job [1960s+] (US)
hummer [1960s+] (US)
knob-job [1960s+] (orig. US)
knobber [1980s+] (US campus)
kowtow chow [1980s+] (US gay)
larking [late 18C-19C]
larro [20C] ('oral' in backslang)
lip-lock [1970s+] (US)
lip service [1970s]
meat whistle [1940s+] (US)
mouth fuck [mid-19C]
pricknic [1980s+] (US gay)
s.m.s. [1990s] (US campus; 'suckle *my* sac')
shiner/shiners [1990s] (from the glistening spittle on
    the penis)
sixty-eight [1970s+] ('you suck me and I'll owe you one')
skull [1970s+] (orig. US Black)
skull fuck [1990s] (US)
skull-buggery [1990s]
slice of ham [20C] (rhy. sl. 'gam' = *gamahuche*)
suck [1920s+]
sucking [1920s+] (orig. US)
white swallow [1990s]

TO FELLATE

blow [1930s+]
blow off [1990s] (US)
blow someone's cookies [1930s+]
blow someone's glass [1970s+]
blow someone's/the pipe [1910s] (US)
blow the skin flute [20C]
brush someone's teeth [1980s+] (US gay)
cap [1960s-70s] (US Black)
clean someone's/the pipe [20C] (US)
cop a bird [1940s] (US)
cop a/one's joint [1960s+] (US)
deep throat [1970s+]
do [1950s+] (US gay)
draw the blinds [1980s+] (US gay; i.e. the foreskin)
draw the curtains [1980s+] (US gay)
drink from the fountain of youth [1990s]
French [late 19C+]
gam/gamb [mid-19C+]
gamahuche [mid-19C+]
   (Greek *gamos*, a wedding or
   Northumbrian dial. *rouched*,
   wrinkled, puckered)

223

skull-buggery

give cone [1980s] (US teen)
give head [1940s+] (orig. US)
hoover/hoover up [1970s+] (orig. US)
kiss [19C]
kiss the worm [1970s+]
kneel at the altar [1960s+] (US prison)
lay the lip [1970s+] (US)
lick log [1990s] (US)
line up on [1910s+]
mouth fuck [1970s+]
play the flute [20C] (US gay)
play the pink oboe [1990s]
play the skin flute [20C]
polish the knob [20C] (US)

224

polish the old German
　　helmet [20C] (US)
prick-lick [1980s+] (US)
put some slobber on the
　　knobber [20C] (US)
smoke the baldy man [1990s]
smoke the big one [1990s]
smoke the blue-veined havana [1990s]
smoke the white owl [1990s]
spit out of the window [1930s+] (gay; spit out
　　one's partner's semen after fellatio)
suck [1920s+]
suck off [1920s+]
swing [1970s+]
talk to the mike [1980s+] (US teen)
tongue lash [1930s+] (US gay)
whip some skull on [1970s+]

'EATING' THE PENIS

bite someone's crank [1960s+]
eat sausage [1980s+] (N.Z.)
eat someone's meat [1920s+]
gnaw the 'nana [1960s+]
gnaw the bone [1990s]
gob the knob [1990s] (US)
gobble [1970s+]
gobble hose [1980s+]
gobble the goo [1910s+] (orig. US)
gobble the gook [1910s+] (orig. US)
gobble the goop [1910s+] (orig. US)
gobble the goose [1910s+] (orig. US)
gum [1980s+] (US gay)
nosh [1950s+]
plate [1950s+] (rhy. sl. 'plates of meat' = 'eat')
suck the sugar-stick [19C]
woof it [1980s+] (US gay)

225

TO BE FELLATED

f.s. [1960s+] (i.e. 'face sit')
get face [1960s+] (orig. US)
get head/skull [1990s]
have one's hat nailed to the ceiling [1910s-30s] (US)
take it any way [1930s-40s]

ORAL SEX: SPECIALITIES

around the world/tongue bath [1960s+] (licking
and sucking the partner's body, including the
genitals and anus)

blood sports [1990s] (cunnilingus on a menstruating
woman)

cherry blossom kiss [1990s] (cunnilingus on a
menstruating woman)

facial [1970s+] (US gay; ejaculating in one's partner's
face)

fifty-fifty [1980s+] (gay; refers to alternating fellatio
and anal sex)

gummer [1990s] (US; fellatio performed by an old
toothless person)

half-and-half [1930s+] (fellatio plus full intercourse
as offered by a prostitute)

high Russian [1960s+] (gay; refers to simultaneous
oral and anal sex)

make the blind see [1980s+] (US gay; fellate an
uncircumcised penis)

pearl necklace [1990s] (drops of semen ejaculated on
to a partner's neck after fellatio)

ride a blind piece [1960s] (gay; fellate an uncircumcised penis)

show tunes [1960s+] (US gay; noises made during sex
or fellatio)

zipper dinner/sex [1960s+] (US gay; very quick
fellatio without even dropping one's trousers)

THE FELLATOR OR FELLATRIX

artiste [1980s+] (US gay)

barbecue [1930s-40s] (US Black; i.e. 'a hot piece of meat')

bumper head [20C] (US)

chickenhead [1960s+] (US Black)

face artist [1970s+] (US Und.)

felicia [1980s+] (US gay; mispron. of 'fellatio')

French active [1950s+] (gay; the person being fellated)

French passive [1950s+] (gay; the person who is fellating)

French by injection [1950s-60s] (gay; describes the
    unusually gifted fellator)

French language expert [1950s+] (gay)

Frenchman [20C]

gap mouth [1990s] (US Black)

glutton for punishment [1970s+] (one who continues to
    fellate even after orgasm has been reached)

head-chick [1930s-40s] (US Black)

head hunter [1980s+] (US)

icing expert [1960s+] (gay; *icing* = semen)

mouser [early 19C-1900s] (a fellatrix who nibbles rather than
    sucks the penis)

skull pussy [1980s+] (US gay)

smoker [1990s]

stool-pigeon [1980s+]
    (US gay; one who loiters in men's toilets to offer fellatio)

THE PENIS 'EATER'

bone-gobbler [20C] (US)
choadsmoker [1960s+] (*choad* = penis)
clarinet-player [1950s] (Aus.)
cocksmoker [1990s] (Can.)
cocksucker [late 19C+] (orig. US)
dicklicker [1960s+]
dicksucker [1970s+] (US)
dicky-licker [1930s+] (orig. US)
flute-player [1950s+] (US)
fluter [1970s+]
gobbledygoo/gobblegoo [1930s-40s] (US)
gobbler [1920s+] (US)
iron jaws [1980s+] (US gay)
knob-gobbler [1960s+]
lick-spigot [18C-19C]
meathound [1960s] (US Black)
mighty mouth [1950s-60s] (camp gay)
mouth-worker [1960s+]
muncher boy [1960s+] (US)
muzzler [1920s-50s]
nob scoffer [1990s]
peter puffer [20C] (US)
peter-eater [1980s+] (US)
piccolo-player [1950s]
raw jaws [1980s+] (US gay; refers to the novice fellator)
scumsucker [1960s+] (orig. US)
sperm burper [1990s]
spigot-sucker [19C]
spunk-gullet [20C]

sucker [late 19C+]
suckster/suckstress [late 19C-1900s]
sword-swallower [late 19C+] (orig. Aus.)

CUNNILINGUS

blow some tunes [1980s+] (US Black)
brush someone's teeth [1980s+] (US Black)
cap [1960s-70s] (US Black)
centerfield on [1930s] (US)
dive [1930s+] (orig. US)
dive in the canyon [1960s+]
face the nation [1970s+] (US Black)
eat someone's flowers [mid-late 19C]
give face [1960s+] (US)
give up one's face [1960s+]
go fish [1960s+]
go south/go way down south in Dixie [1950s] (US)
go under the house [1970s]
go/come lickety-split [1970s+]
gorilla in the washing machine [1970s] (US Black)
grin in the canyon/the canyon of love [1960s+]
grin up the valley [1960s+]
hunt the anchovy [1960s+]
kiss the baby/baby in the boat [1930s]
lap/lap up [1920s+]
lick a box [1990s] (orig. W.I.)
lick the holy ground [1990s]
pearl dive [1960s+] (US; the 'pearl' is the clitoris)

229

quimling [1990s]
scalp [1970s] (US Black)
slop at the hog trough [1930s] (US Black)
sneeze in the cabbage/canyon [1960s+]
swap spit [20C]
talk to the canoe-driver [1960s] (US; play on 'cunnilingus')
tongue [1930s+]
whistle in the dark [1960s+] (US)
yodel in the canyon/the canyon
    of love [1960s+]
yodel up the valley [1960s+]

230

'EATING' THE VAGINA

chew fish/the fish [1940s+] (US)
chow box [1990s] (US)
dine at the Y [1940s+] (orig. US)
eat at the Y [1950s+] (US)
eat box lunch at the Y [1950s+] (US)
eat cheese [1940s+] (orig. US Black)
eat fish/the fish [1940s+] (US)
eat out [1960s+] (US)
eat pie [1980s+]
eat pussy [1950s+]
fress [20C] (orig. US; Yiddish 'to eat')
go downstairs for breakfast [1970s] (Aus.)
lunch at the lazy Y [1950s+] (US)

MUFF-DIVING

chew the carpet [1980s+] (US)
dive a muff [1940s+] (orig. US)
dive in the bushes [1960s+]
drink at the fuzzy cup [1970s+] (US Black)
eat a furburger [1980s+] (US)
eat hair pie [1960s+]
growl at the badger [1990s]
growl in her busby [1930s]
have a moustache [20C]
muff [1960s+] (US)
muff-dive [1940s+] (orig. US)
muff-nosh [1940s+] (orig. US)
munch the carpet [1980s+] (US)
sip at the fuzzy cup [1970s+] (US Black)
wear the beard [1990s]

THE CUNNILINCTOR

cannibal [1960s+] (US Black)
carpet-muncher [1980s+] (US campus)
cat [1950s+]
cocksucker [late 19C+] (orig. US)
fish queen [1960s+] (from the 'fishy' vagina)
fresser [20C] (US; Yiddish 'eater')
gash-eater [1970s+]
growl-biter [late 19C+]
head jockey [1950s+]
high diver [1930s+]
lap-lover [1990s]

lapper [1920s+]
lick-twat [17C-19C]
lipkisser [1960s+] (US)
mickey-muncher [1980s+] (Aus.)
muff-diver [1930s+] (US)
muffer [1960s+] (US)
rug-muncher [1980s+] (US campus)
trapeze artist [1930s+]

SOIXANTE-NEUF

breakfast of champions [1990s] (from the
    slogan of the US breakfast cereal Wheaties)
flip-flop [1960s-70s]
flying sixty-nine [20C]
halvsies [1980s]
heads and tails [late 19C-1950s] (Aus.)
hoop-snake [1960s-70s]
loop-the-loop [1970s+]
sixty-nine [late 19C+]

Kinky Sex

THE ORGY

all in one [1970s]
ballum rancum [late 17C-late 19C]
bang [1980s+] (US Black)
buff-ball [late 19C]
bumfest [1990s] (a homosexual orgy)
bunch punch [1970s+] (orig. US campus)
circus [1950s+] (US)
clusterfuck [1960s+] (orig. US)
cluster-screw [1970s] (US)
fuck-a-rama [1960s+] (orig. US; a long orgy)
fuck-in [1960s-70s] (US hippie)
fuckathon [1960s+] (orig. US; a long orgy)
fuckfest [1970s] (US)
gang roll [late 19C] (US)
gang-screw [1950s+]
gang-splash [1960s+] (Aus.)
gangbang [1950s+]
group grope
    [1960s+]

love-in [1960s+] (US)
party [1960s+] (an encounter involving two or more women
    and one man)
pig party [1960s]
ring around the rosy [1960s+] (US gay)
Roman culture [1960s+]
Roman night [1960s+] (gay)
Russian salad party [1950s-60s] (an orgy in which
    everyone is drenched in baby oil)
skeeze [1980s+] (US Black; to have an orgy)
swing/swing party [1970s+] (orig. US; esp. involving the
    swapping of husbands and wives)
team cream [1960s+] (gay)
threesome [1990s]

THE ORGY: PARTICIPANTS

buttered bun [20C] (a woman who has had sex with one
    man and is about to repeat the act with a new partner)
double-barrelled gun [20C] (a woman who is
    amenable to group sex involving vaginal and anal
    intercourse)
fore and after [19C] (a woman who is amenable to
    group sex involving vaginal and anal intercourse)
groupie [1960s+] (a devotee of group sex)
Roman historian [1960s+] (an enthusiast for orgies)
splash [1980s+] (woman participating in multiple
    intercourse)
wet deck [late 19C+] (Can./US; a woman who engages
    in serial sex acts)

ANAL SEX

assfucking [1950s+]
bit of brown [mid-19C+]
brown [mid-19C]
budli-budli [20C]
buttfuck [1960s+]
Greek [1930s+]
Irish way [20C] (heterosexual anal intercourse)
keister [1930s-60s] (US prison)

TO PERFORM ANAL INTERCOURSE

ask for the ring [1950s+]
brown/do a brown [1920s+] (orig. US)
bull [1980s+] (W.I.)
bust some booty [1980s+] (US Black)
buy the ring [1960s+]
fudge [1970s+] (US)
get some brown/brown sugar [1970s+]
go Greek [1980s] (US)
goose [late 19C+]
go up the old dirt road [1910s+]
jacksy jockey [1990s] (an aficionado of anal sex,
    either gay or straight)
leather [1930s+]
molly [mid-18C]
pack [1980s+] (US campus)
plug [1960s+]
shoot one's star [1970s] (US Black)

ANILINGUS

bilingual [1980s+] (US gay)
brown job [1960s+]
brown wings [1950s+]
ream job [1970s]
rim job [1950s+]
rim queen [1950s+] (i.e. an anilinguist)
ringpiece licker [1990s] (i.e. an anilinguist)
tossed salad [1990s] (US Black teen; anilingus enhanced by
    the application of jam or syrup)

237

A BRIEF LEXICON OF UNUSUAL SEX

b & d [1960s+] (bondage and discipline)

bottom [1960s+] (the passive partner in S & M sex)

catcher [1950s+] (the passive partner in S & M, gay or straight sex)

cottage crawl [1950s+] (to frequent public lavatories for sex)

do a fruit salad [1980s+] (US campus; to expose one's genitals in public)

English [1960s-70s] (US; sado-masochistic)

English culture [1960s+] (sex advertisements for b & d)

English disease [1960s+] (erotic flagellation)

English guidance [1960s+] (b & d)

felch [1960s] (usu. gay; to lick out the semen from the anus of someone who has just enjoyed anal inter-course)

felch queen [1950s+] (a gay man who is stimulated by faecal matter)

fist fuck [1970s] (gay; to insert one's hand and forearm into someone's anus or vagina)

fladge queen [1950s+] (a gay man who enjoys flagellation)

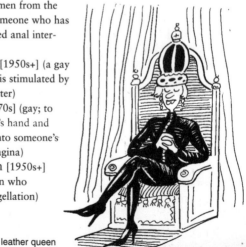

leather queen

flogster [late 19C+] (one who enjoys flagellation)

game room [1960s+] (a torture chamber for S & M sex)

get some cold comfort [1980s] (to have sexual relations with a corpse)

get some duke [1970s] (to have someone's fist or fingers pushed into one's anus; *dukie* = excrement)

golden shower [1960s+] (orig. US gay; urolagnia)

golden shower queen [1960s+] (a homosexual who enjoys being urinated on)

govern [1960s+] (to take the active role in S & M sex)

jemima suit [1990s] (a leather or rubber suit with strategically placed holes over the erogenous zones)

leather bar [1960s+] (US gay; a bar used by leather fetishists)

leather boy [1960s+] (gay; gay male leather fetishist)

leather freak [1960s+] (US; a leather fetishist)

leather queen [1960s+] (a gay man who likes dressing in leather)

make a milk run [1990s] (US gay; to hang about public lavatories looking for sex)

pitch [1960s+] (gay; to take the active role in S & M sex)

roughhouse [1960s+] (US; to enjoy S & M sex)

r/s [1970s+] ('*rough stuff*')

rubber queen [1960s+] (a rubber fetishist)

sad-ass [1960s+] (US gay; a sadist)

sadie and maisie [1960s+] (sado-masochism)

sado-maso [1970s] (US; a sado-masochist)

scatting [1960s] (defecating on one's partner's face)

service station [1980s+] (US gay; a public lavatory used for sexual assignations)

shrimper [1960s+] (a foot fetishist)

slap queen [1950s-60s] (gay; a gay man given to heavy use of make-up)

slaves and masters [1960s+] (US; sadists and masochists)

spit-fuck [1960s+] (gay; penetration of the anus by the penis, fingers or fist where the only lubricant is spit)

tightbuck [1950s+] (the foetal position, popular for tying up participants in S & M sex)

toe-jam queen [1960s] (US gay; a gay male foot fetishist)

toe queen [1950s+] (a foot fetishist)

top [1960s+] (the dominant partner in a gay S & M relationship)

top man [1960s+] (the dominant partner in a gay S & M relationship)

underwear [1960s+] (a soiled underwear fetishist)

warm the husband's supper [19C] (to stand in front of the fire with lifted skirts)

water sports [1960s+] (urinating on a partner for sexual stimulation)

w/s [1960s+] (*water sports*)

Gay and Bi

HOMOSEXUALITY

arse/ass banditry [20C]
bum banditry [1960s+]
Dorian love [20C] (gay; from Oscar Wilde's novella
    The Picture of Dorian Gray)
duncarring [late 17C-18C] (from *dunnaken*, a privy)
faggotry [1910s+]
the life [1950s+] (gay)
nastiness [1950s] (W.I.)
Oscar Wildeing [1900s]
sapphism [1950s+] (i.e. lesbianism; from Sappho,
    the 'godmother' of lesbianism)
sugar [1990s] (US Black)

HOMOSEXUAL

bent [1950s+]
chichi [1960s+]
gay [1950s+] (orig. US)
Greek [1930s+]
Hershey [1970s+] (US; the brand name of Hershey bars)

HIGH AND LOW GREEK

Low Greek [1960s+] (gay; refers to heterosexual inter-
    course, the vagina being lower down than the anus)
High Greek [1960s+] (gay; refers to homosexual inter-
    course, the anus being higher up than the vagina)

Irish by birth but Greek by injection [1960s+]
lavender [1920s+] (orig. US)
queer [1920s+]
so [late 19C-1950s]

THE HOMOSEXUAL MAN

agfay [1940s-70s] (Pig Latin 'fag')
badger [1990s] (US)
bag [1920s+] (esp. an unattractive or passive gay man)
balloon-knot bandit [1990s]
bardache [mid-16C-early 18C] (Arabic *bardaj*, 'a slave')
beachcomber [1990s] (pun on 'log-pusher')
bender [1930s+]
blow-boy [1930s+] (US)
bone smuggler [1990s]
bone-stroker [1990s]
bowler from the pavilion end [1990s]
budli-budli [20C] (Urdu 'change')
buller [1980s+] (Black)
camp [1930s] (orig. US)
cat [1950s+] (Aus.; a passive male homosexual)
chemise-lifter [1960s+]
cocksucker [1940s+]
double-barrelled ghee [1950s-60s] (gay)
eerquay [1930s-40s] (US; Pig Latin 'queer')
fag [1920s+] (orig. US)
fagola [1960s] (US)
foop [20C] (backslang 'poof')

243

THE OLDER GAY MAN

afghan [1960s] (US gay)
dad [1950s]
daddy [1930s+] (orig. US)
dirty dowager [1950s-60s] (gay; an unkempt
    older gay man)
dowager [1950s+] (gay)
grand duchess [1950s+] (gay)
mary worthless [1940s+] (gay; an ageing,
    unattractive gay man)
over-ripe fruit [1950s-60s] (gay)
papa [1950s+]
pension-book crowd [1950s-60s]
    (gay; i.e. older gay men as a group)
queen [late 19C+]
sugar mama [1980s+] (US gay)
toad [20C] (US gay; an unattractive older gay man)
troll [1980s+] (US gay; an unattractive older gay man)

freak [20C] (orig. US Black)
fuckboy [1970s+] (a passive male homosexual)
funny man [1970s+] (US Black)
gay [1940s+]
gay boy [1950s+] (US)
gayola [1980s+] (US)
green and yellow fellow [late 19C] (from the colours
    associated with the Aesthetic Movement of the 1890s)
Hollywood hustler [1950s+] (US)
homo [1920s+]

THE YOUNGER GAY MAN

capon [1930s-40s]
cupcake [1960s+] (US gay)
gal-boy [late 19C+] (US)
ganymede [1910s-40s] (US)
lilywhite [late 19C-1900s]
pretty [1930s+] (gay)
princess [1960s] (gay)
queerbait [1950s+]
trug [16C-early 18C] (UK Und.)
twinkie [1970s+] (US gay)

245

inspector of manholes [1930s+]
Jesuit [mid-16C]
joey [20C] (Aus.; lit. 'a young kangaroo')
john-and-john [late 18C-mid-19C]
joy boy [20C] (US)
Kinsey 6 [1950s] ('completely homosexual' as categorized
   in the Kinsey Report)
kisser [20C] (i.e. 'ass kisser')
knick-knack [1960s+] (US; lit. 'a trinket')
man-eater [1940s+]
mandrake [early 17C+]
mole [late 19C-1910s]
morphodite/morphodyte/morphodyke [18C+]
one [1930s-60s]
one of those [late 19C]
one of us [1930s+]

oofterpa [1940s] (Pig Latin 'poofter')
pickle kisser [1990s]
pipe smoker [1990s]
poggler [20C]
pole pleaser [20C] (US)
woman [1960s+] (US prison)
poofter/poofdah/poofta [late 19C+] (orig. Aus.)
puff [20C]
punk [20C]
queer [1920s+]
semen demon [20C] (US)
shirtlifter [1960s+] (orig. Aus.)
short-arm bandit [1960s-70s] (*short-arm* = penis)
skin-diver [20C]
sod [mid-19C+]
sperm burper [1990s]
sweetcorn shiner [1990s]
tonk [1940s+] (Aus.)
tootle-merchant [1980s+]
town shift [mid-17C-mid-18C]
trouser bandit [20C]
tubesteak tarzan [1990s]
turd-burglar [1960s+] (orig. Aus.)
undercover man [20C]
weirdie [1960s]

'BROWN' TERMS

brown artist [1950s+]
brown dirt cowboy [1990s]
brown pipe [1990s]

Cadbury's canal boat cruiser [1990s]
Cadbury's canal engineer [1990s]
chocky jockey [1990s]
chocolate runway pilot [1990s]
chocolate speedway rider [1990s]
chutney farmer [1990s]
cocoa-shunter [1990s]
fudge-nudger [1990s]
fudge-packer [20C] (US)
hitchhiker on the Hershey highway [20C] (US)
Marmite driller [1990s]
Marmite miner [1990s]
peanut buffer [1990s]
peanut-packer [1950s+] (US)
pilot of the chocolate runway [1990s]
sausage jockey [1990s] (US)
sausage smuggler [1990s]
visitor to Vegemite valley [1990s]

247

VARIOUS ANAL TERMS

anal astronaut [1990s]
arse pirate [1990s]
ass boy [1990s] (US)
ass burglar [1970s+]
b.b. [20C] (i.e. '*bum-boy*')
back-door commando [1990s]
back-door kicker [1990s]
battie-boy [20C] (orig. W.I.)
batty bwoy [1960s+] (W.I./UK Black teen)
booty-buffer [1990s]

boretto-man [early 18C] (Ital. 'little borer')
breechloader [1910s]
bufu [1980s+] (orig. US; i.e. 'buttfucker')
buftie/bufty [20C]
bufty-boy [20C]
buggeranto [early 18C]
bum boy [19C+]
bum chum [1990s]
bum plumber [1990s]
bum-robber [late 19C+]
bummer [1970s]
bummer-boy [1970s]
bunny boy [1940s+] (S.Afr.)
cackpipe cosmonaut [1990s]
chuff adder [1960s] (play on 'puff adder')
chuff chum [1990s]
colon choker [1990s]
dinner masher [1990s]
dirt-tamper [1970s]
donut-puncher [1990s] (US)

248

COVERT

angel with a dirty face [1960s]
block boy [1990s]
closet [1950s+] (orig. gay)
closet case [1950s+] (gay)
closet queen [1960s+] (gay)
Trojan horse [1960s+] (US gay)

TO REVEAL ONE'S HOMOSEXUALITY

come out of the closet [1960s+] (orig. US)
discover one's gender [1950s+] (gay)
drop one's beads [1950s+] (gay)
go over [1910s+] (Aus.)
turn the corner [20C]

eye doctor [1950s+]
freckle-puncher [1960s+]
haemorrhoid hitman [1990s]
hip-hitter [1960s]
hole-filler [1990s]
hoop stretcher [1990s]
hula raider [1990s]
indorser [late 18C-19C]
jobby jouster [1990s]
log-cabin raider [1990s]
log-pusher [1990s]
mud-packer [20C] (US)
navigator of the windward passage [1990s]
nudger [1990s] (US)
pile-driver [1960s-70s]
poo percolator [1990s]
poo pusher [1990s]
poo-packer [1990s]
poo-stabber [1990s]
prune-pusher [1950s-60s]
putty pusher [1990s]

THE HOMOSEXUAL MAN IN RHYMING SLANG

rhyming with *queer*
ginger [1920s+]
King Lear [20C]
shandy [20C] (i.e. 'chandelier')

rhyming with *poof* or *poofter*
cloven hoofter [20C] (Aus.)
horse's hoof [1950s+]
iron [1930s+]
iron hoof [1930s+]
jam duff [20C]
nellie/nelly duff [20C]
nice enough [20C]
woofter [1980s+]
woolly woofter [1980s+]

rhyming with *queen*
haricot [1960s+] (Aus.)
in-between [20C] (Aus.)
pork and bean [1960s+] (Aus.)

rhyming with *nance*
song and dance [1910s-30s]

rhyming with *catamite*
dyna [1960s] (i.e. 'dynamite')

rhyming with *cock*
hock [20C]

rhyming with *bent*
Stoke on Trent [1970s+]

CLAPHAM COMMON

rear seat gunner [1990s]
rectal/rectum ranger [1990s]
rimadona [1960s] (gay; pun on 'rimming')
ring master [1990s]
ring raider [1990s]
rump ranger [1950s+]
scatman [1990s]
shit-stabber [1960s+]
shunter [1990s]
skid-pipe plumber [1990s]
stem-wheeler [20C] (US)
stir-shit [late 19C-1900s]
tailgunner [1960s+] (US)
tan-track rider [1930s+] (orig. Aus.)
tan-tracker [1930s+] (orig. Aus.)
uphill gardener [1990s]
windjammer [20C] (Aus.)

EFFEMINATE

angel [19C]
annie [1950s]
auntie [1930s+] (US gay)
betty [19C]
bitch [1930s+] (gay)
boong-moll [1930s+] (Aus.; lit. 'man-woman')
brilliant [20C] (gay)
broad boy [20C] (lit. 'girl-boy')
broken wrist [1960s-70s]
bruce [1940s-70s] (gay term of address)
buttercup [20C]

PASSIVE

bottom man [1950s+]
brownie [1960s] (US gay)
browning queen [1940s+] (US gay)
hole [1960s+] (US)
less than nothing [20C] (US Black)
mampala/mampala-man [20C] (W.I.)
mattress-muncher [1960s+] (orig. Aus.)
pussyboy [1950s]
quean [late 19C+] .
receiver [20C]

butterfly [1940s] (US Black)
charlie [1940s+] (Aus.; rhy. sl. *Charlie Wheeler* = 'sheila')
cream puff [1960s+]
daisy [1940s+]
ethel [1920s+]
faddle [late 19C] (lit. 'a fussy person')
fairy [late 19C+] (orig. US)
fancy man [1970s+] (US)
faygele/feygele [20C] (US; Yiddish 'a little bird')
fembo [1980s+] (US campus; i.e. a 'female Rambo')
femme/fem [1960s+] (US)
flamer [1960s+] (US campus)
flip [1980s+] (US Black)
flit [1930s+] (US)
flower [20C]
foxy lady [20C]

frit [1940s-60s] (US)
gal-boy [late 19C+] (US)
gina la salsa [1950s] (camp gay; an effeminate Italian homosexual)
girl-boy [late 19C+] (US)
gladys [1950s-60s] (camp gay)
gussie [late 19C+] (Aus.)
hasie [1960s+] (S.Afr.; lit. 'a hare')
hen [20C] (W.I.)
hesh [20C] (i.e. 'he-she')
himmer [1950s] (i.e 'him-her')
huckle [1900s] (US)
jessie [1920s+]
lavender boy [1920s+]
lavender cowboy [1990s]
lightfoot [20C]

MACHO

bull [1960s-70s] (US)
butch [1930s+] (orig. US)
butch number [mid-20C] (gay)
hairy Mary [1960s+] (US gay)
hawk [1960s+] (S. Afr.)
jailhouse daddy [1950s-60s] (US prison)
jocker [1910s] (US prison)
pitcher [1960s+] (the dominant partner)
steamer [1950s-60s] (gay man who prefers passive partners)
truck-driver [1950s+] (US Black)

limp wrist/wrister [1950s+] (orig. US)
lollipop [1920s-60s] (US)
madge-cove [early 18C-mid-19C] (*Madge* = Margaret)
madge-cull [late 18C-mid-19C]
mama [1940s-70s] (US)

THE HOMOSEXUAL MAN: SPECIALISTS

church mouse [1960s] (a gay man who attends
  crowded churches to fondle potential sex partners)
daughter [1960s+] (a gay man brought into the gay
  world by a gay friend or 'mother')
drip-dry lover [1960s+] (US gay; a gay man with a
  small penis)
fantail [1960s] (US; a promiscuous prison homosexual)
hair fairy [1960s+] (US; an effeminate gay man with
  long or styled hair)
ki-ki/kiki [1930s-60s] (US; a gay man who indulges in
  simultaneous genital and oral sex)
mother [1940s+] (US gay; a gay man who introduces
  another gay man or 'daughter' into the gay world)
nick-nack/nic-nac [1960s+] (US; esp. a promiscuous
  homosexual)
piss elegant [1950s+] (an ostentatious homosexual)
pisshole bandit [1960s+] (a gay man who solicits in
  lavatories)
screaming fairy/queen [1940s+] (an ostentatiously
  effeminate gay man)
sea pussy [1980s+] (a gay sailor)

margery [mid-19C+]

mary ann [late 19C+]

maud [1940s+]

minty/mintee/mintie [1910s-70s] (US gay)

Miss It [1950s+]

Miss Molly [early 18C-1920s]

Miss Nancy [early 19C-1920s]

Miss Thing [1950s+] (orig. US gay; used as a greeting between gay men)

moll [1920s-40s] (US)

molly [early 18C-1900s]

molly-boy [early 18C-1920s]

mouse [1930s] (US Und.)

nance [20C]

nancy [late 19C+] (orig. US)

nancy boy [1950s+]

nellie/nelly [1910s+]

omee-polone/-paloney [late 19C+] (Polari 'man-woman')

Oscar [1900s-50s] (US; from *Oscar* Wilde)

pantyman [20C] (W.I.)

pixie [late 19C]

powder puff [1920s+]

pretty-boy [20C]

princess [1960s] (gay)

pure silk [1960s] (US Black)

rabbit [1940s+] (S.Afr.)

royalie/royaly [1900s-20s]

she-male [20C]

she-man [20C]

sheena [1950s-60s] (camp gay)

shim [20C]

sissie [late 19C+]
sissy-boy (US)
sissy pants [20C]
sister [1940s-60s] (US; a platonic friend of a gay man)
skippy [1930s-40s] (US Black)
smockface [19C] (lit. 'one with a smooth face')
soft [mid-19C+]
soft boy [1980s+] (Black)
soft sucker [1980s+] (US Black)
sweet [1970s] (US Black)
swish [1930s+] (orig. US)
three-legged beaver [20C]
tooti-frooti [1960s+] (US Black)
triss/trizz [1950s+] (Aus.)
waffle [1970s+] (US Und.)
woman-man [20C] (W.I.)

FRUITS

fruit [1930s+]
fruitcake [1930s+]
fruiter [1910s+] (US)
fruit for monkeys [1930s+] (US)
fruit loop [1980s+] (US campus)
fruit-fly [1950s+]
fruit-plate [1930s+] (US)
juicy fruit [1930s] (US Black)
pineapple [1960s-70s]
ripe fruit [1980s+] (US gay; someone who has recently
    discovered their homosexuality)

THE LESBIAN

amy-john [20C]
bean flicker [1990s] (*bean* = clitoris)
bull bitch [1960s+] (US)
bull-dyke [1920s+] (a masculine lesbian)
butch [1930s+] (a masculine lesbian)
carpet-muncher [1980s+] (US campus)
charlie [1940s+] (Aus.)
clam smacker [1990s] (US)
clithopper [1960s] (a promiscuous lesbian)
donut-bumper [20C] (US)
douchebag [1940s+] (US)
Dutch girl [1930s+] (pun on 'dyke')
dyke [1930s+]
faggot [1950s] (US)
fairy lady [1940s-50s] (US)
femme/fem [1960s+] (a feminine lesbian)
finger artist [1940s-70s] (US Black)
fuzz bumper [1980s+] (US campus)
gal officer [1940s-50s] (US Black)
gaychick [1980s+] (US gay)
goose girl [1910s]
gusset-nuzzler [1990s]
harpy [1970s] (US Black)
jasper [1950s+] (US prison/Black)
ki-ki/kiki [1930s-60s] (US)
lady-lover [1930s+]
lemon [1980s+] (Aus.)
lemonade [1980s+] (Aus.)
leslie [1950s+] (Aus.)

lizzie/Lizzie [1940s+]

l.u.g. [1980s+] (orig. US campus; *l*esbian *u*ntil *g*raduation,
    denotes a female student who is not necessarily a lesbian,
    but who experiments with lesbian politics and culture)

malflor [1960s+] (US)

muffer [1960s+] (US)

nellie/nelly [1970s+] (US campus)

raleigh bike [20C] (rhy. sl. = 'dyke')

rug-muncher [1980s+] (US campus)

sappho [1950s+]

she-he [1940s-60s] (US)

slut-puppy [1980s+] (US campus)

sucker [late 19C+]

thespian [1970s]

tom [late 19C]

tootsie [20C] (Aus.)

tootsey-wootsey/tootsie-wootsie [20C] (Aus.)

tunaface [1990s]

vegetable [1980s+]
    (US gay)

wicker [1980s+]
    (Black)

zamie [1950s+]
    (W.I.)

zamie girl
    [1950s+] (W.I.)

drink from both taps

BISEXUAL

AC/DC [1940s+]
ace-deuce [1970s] (US)
acey-deucey [1970s+] (US Black)
AM/FM [1980s+]
ambidextrous [1930s+]
ambisextrous [1920s+] (US)
double-gaited [1920s-60s] (US)
greedy [1990s]
half-and-half [1930s+] (US campus)
neither Arthur or Martha [20C]
versatile [1950s-60s]

THE BISEXUAL PERSON

bicycle [1970s+]
bipe [1960s+] (US)
combo [1980s+] (US campus)
double-life man [20C]
dunt [1980s+] (US campus; *dick* + *cunt*)
flip-flop [20C] (US prison)
ki-ki/kiki [1930s-60s] (US)
switch-hitter [1950s+] (US)

TO BE BISEXUAL

bat and bowl [1950s+]
drink from both taps [1990s]
plug in both ways [1970s+]
swing both ways [1960s+]

Buying It

PROSTITUTION

bashing [1930s+]
business [1900s-60s] (US)
fancy work [late 19C]
the game [1930s+] (US Black)
the life [20C] (orig. US)
loose-coat game [16C]
pros [20C]
pussy game [1960s+] (US)
social E [late 19C] (i.e. 'social evil')
suburb trade [late 19C]
way of life [early 19C]

THE FEMALE PROSTITUTE

bird [mid-19C+] (a tough and experienced prostitute)
blowen [late 17C-mid-19C] (Romani *beluni*, 'a sister in
    debauchery')
blower [18C-19C]
blowse/blowze [late 16C-early 18C]
broad [1910s+] (US)
broadie [1930s+] (US)
call-girl [1930s+] (orig. US)
charlie [1940s+] (Aus.; rhy. sl. *Charlie Wheeler* = 'sheila')
dasher [late 18C-late 19C] (a flashy prostitute)
flirtina cop-all [mid-late 19C]
game [late 17C-early 19C] (refers to a group of prostitutes in
    a brothel)

hooker [mid-19C+] (orig. US)
jack's delight [19C] (jack tar's, i.e. a sailor's delight)
jamette [20C] (W.I.; French sl. *jeanette*, a whore)
jay [16C-1970s+] (a flashy prostitute)
laced mutton [17C-mid-19C] (from the lacings of her corset)
maggie [17C; 1930s]
mort [mid-16C-late 19C]
mud-kicker [1930s+] (orig. US; i.e. she walks the streets in
    all weathers)
pony [1960s+] (i.e. one who is 'ridden')
prossie [1930s+] (orig. Aus.)
prostie [1930s+] (US)
raw meat [late 18C+]
sporting lady [mid-19C] (US)
tail [late 18C-mid-19C]
tart [late 19C+]
vroe/vrow [early 17C-19C]

THE PART-TIME PROSTITUTE

B-girl [1930s-60s] (US; abbr. 'bar girl')
bar-hog [1960s] (US)
charity chippy [1930s+] (an amateur prostitute or one who
    undercuts her peers)
charity moll [1940s+] (Aus.; an amateur prostitute or one
    who undercuts her peers)
chippie/chippy [late 19C+] (orig. US)
cracked pitcher [mid-18C-mid-19C]
dollymop [mid-late 19C]
ewe-mutton [18C]
for-free [1940s] (orig. US)

263

half-brass [1940s+] (woman who associates with
    prostitutes but is not a 'working girl' herself)
half-squarie [1910s-50s]
hoove [1990s] (US Black)
messer [1910s+]
omo [1960s+] (i.e. 'old *man* out'; the placing of a packet
    of the washing powder *Omo* in the woman's window
    indicates that her husband is away at sea and that
    she is available for sex)
privateer [late 19C-1910s]
tottie fay [late 19C+]
tottie fie [late 19C+]
tottie hardbake [late 19C+]
V-girl [1940s] (US; V = Victory, denotes a woman willing
    to have sex with servicemen for patriotic reasons)
weekend ho [1960s+]
weekend warrior [1960s+]

THE YOUNG PROSTITUTE

chicken [late 18C-mid-19C]
downy bit [mid-19C]
flapper [late 19C-1910s] (orig. US)
flipper [late 19C-1910s] (orig. US)
fresh fish [mid-19C+]
fresh greens [mid-late 19C]
fresh meat [19C+]
game pullet [18C]
giggler [early 18C-19C]
giglet [early 18C-19C]

goglet [early 18C-19C]
gold-digger [1910s-20s] (US)
green goose [16C]
kid leather [mid-19C]
kinchin/kitchin mort [mid-late 16C] (UK Und.)
mystery [1930s+]
punk [late 16C-1900s]
trat [late 19C-1900s] (backslang 'tart')

THE EXPERIENCED OR OLD PROSTITUTE

buss beggar [17C-19C] (i.e. she 'begs for a kiss')
dragon [1950s-60s]
mort wap-apace [16C-early 19C] (UK Und.;
    lit. 'girl fuck-fast')
vet [1930s+] (abbr. 'veteran')

265

THE WORN-OUT PROSTITUTE

fleabag [1960s+] (US)
fourpenny [late 19C-1900s]
garbage can [1920s-60s] (US)
hard leg [1940s+] (US Black)
Jodrell [1950s+] (rhy.sl. 'a wank'; i.e. no better than
    masturbation)
pitcher-bawd [late 17C-18C]
second-hand Sue [1940s-50s]
tank [1910s] (from the bulky ugliness of early tanks)
trumpery [late 18C-early 19C] (lit. 'valueless goods')

LONDON LADIES

Bankside lady [17C]
City Road African [late 19C-1900s]
Covent Garden lady [18C]
Covent Garden nun [18C]
Drury Lane vestal [mid-18C-early 19C]
Fleet Street dove [19C]
Fleet Street houri [19C]
Fulham virgin [19C]
Haymarket ware [19C]
Pickethatch vestal [late 18C-early 19C]
St John's Wood dona [19C]
St John's Wood vestal [19C]
Whetstone park deer [17C-18C]

TO WORK AS A PROSTITUTE

accommodate [19C]
bash [1930s+]
battle [late 19C+] (Aus.)
bump [1980s+] (W.I./Baham.)
carry a broom at the masthead [19C] (from the naval
    tradition of hoisting a broom to signify 'the ship has
    been sold')
catch [late 19C+] (US Black)
crack it for a quid [1960s+] (Aus.; *crack* = to open, in this
    case the legs)

do a bit of business [mid-19C+]
flutter a skirt [late 19C-1900s]
freelance [1960s+] (i.e. to work without a pimp)
get up to tricks [19C]
go sparrow-catching [19C]
hawk one's brawn [1970s+] (Aus.)
hawk one's brown [20C] (to work as a male prostitute)
hawk one's fork [20C] (Aus.; the *fork* being the junction
     of the legs)
hawk one's mutton [19C+]
hook [1940s+]
hustle [late 19C] (US)
hustle one's bustle [1930s-40s]
lead a gay life [mid-late 19C]
moll [1950s] (US)
peddle one's hips [1920s-40s]
peddle pussy [1960s+]
pick fares [20C] (W.I./Bdos.; she gives her clients a 'ride')
prank [late 16C]
put it about [1970s+]
rat out [20C] (W.I.)
sit on one's stuff [1970s] (US Black)
sling fish [1980s+] (US)
sling pussy [1960s+] (US)
tom/tom it around [1930s+]
tread one's shoe awry [mid-19C]
turn tricks [20C]
wag one's bottom [late 19C+]
walk the piazzas [18C] (i.e. of Covent Garden, London)
work a door [1920s+]

THE GAY MALE PROSTITUTE

ass pro/aspro/asspro [1920s+] (Aus./US)
bitch [1930s+] (gay)
boulevard boy [1970s+]
boy [1960s+]
buff boy [20C]
burton [1960s-70s] (rhy. sl. *Burton*-on-Trent = 'bent')
business boy [20C]
c.o.d. [1960s+] (i.e. '*c*ash *o*n *d*elivery')
call-boy [1970s+]
capon [1930s-40s] (lit. a 'gelded cock')
career boy [20C]
cash-ass [1960s+]
chick [1940s+]
clip queen [1940s] (US gay; a gay male prostitute who
    specializes in robbing clients)
coin collector [20C]
College Street solicitor [1940s-60s] (Aus.)
come-on boy [1910s+] (a gay male prostitute who
    specializes in robbing clients)
commercial [1960s+] (Aus. gay)
commercial queer [20C]
daffodil [1930s-70s]
dick peddler [1960s+]
dilly boy [1950s+] (a teenage male prostitute working
    around Piccadilly Circus, London)
dollar-an-inch man [1960s+] (US gay; one who claims
    his penis is so large he could get rich by charging
    fellating clients by the inch)
dolly boy [1970s+] (orig. gay)

girl [late 18C-late 19C] (US)
he-whore [20C]
holemonger [late 19C]
holer [late 19C]
knob polisher [1960s+]
knobber [1970s+] (US)
maud [1940s+]
nigh enough [1920s-30s] (rhy. sl. = 'puff')
party boy [1960s+] (US)
prick peddler [1960s+]
raggedy android [1950s-60s] (camp gay; an unsuccessful
    and impoverished male prostitute)
rent [1930s+]
rent boy [1960s+]
renter [late 19C+]
sporting goods [20C]
minion of the suburbs
    [late 16C-late 17C]
Susan Saliva [1950s-70s]
    (camp gay;
    he specialises in
    fellatio and therefore
    'lives by his spits')
tart [1930s+] (gay)
trade [1930s+] (gay)
two-way man [1930s+] (one
    who is amenable to an
    active or passive role in
    anal sex or fellatio)

269

THE BROTHEL

bang [1920s+] (Aus.)

big number [mid-19C-1900s] (Parisian brothels sported extra-large street numbers)

birdcage [1920s] (US)

bordello [late 16C-18C]

bullpen [mid-19C-1930s] (US)

cab [early-mid-19C]

call flat [1910s-20s] (US)

cat wagon [19C-1960s] (US; a travelling brothel)

clap-trap [20C]

convent [mid-18C]

corinth [early 17C-mid-19C] (the Greek city of Corinth was renowned for its debauchery)

Covent Garden nunnery [18C] (Covent Garden in London was a centre for brothels)

cowbay [mid-late 19C] (the brothel area of Cow Bay, New York)

cowyard [late 19C-1910s] (US)

cunny warren [18C]

Cyprian arbour [early 17C] (Cyprus, birthplace of Venus)

free-and-easy [mid-late 19C] (US)

Frenchery [mid-19C+]

fuckery [19C]

girlery [19C]

gunboat [1940s] (US; a riverboat used as a brothel)

hummum [late 17C-19C] (lit. 'a Turkish bath')

juke [1930s+] (US)

meat fancier's [19C]

nautch [late 19C-1940s] (US)

nautchery [late 19C-1940s] (US)

nunnery [late 16C-early 19C]

pheasantry [19C-1900s] (*pheasant* = promiscuous woman)

place of sixpenny sinfulness [19C] (a suburban brothel)

rap club [1970s] (US)

rap studio [1970s] (US)

red lamp [late 19C]

red lattice/grate [16C]

rookery [early 19C]

timothy [1950s+] (Aus.; rhy. sl. *timothy grass* = arse)

warren [late 17C-early 19C]

THE 'HOUSE'

accommodation house [19C]

badger house [mid-19C-1900s] (US; a brothel that
    specialises in robbing its clients)

bat-house [20C] (Aus.; lit. 'whore house')

bawdy-ken [19C]

bed-house [1920s-30s] (US Black)

boogie house/joint [1930s-70s] (US Black)

cab joint [1930s+] (orig. US)

call house [late 19C+]

casa [late 18C-1900s]

cat-house [1930s+] (US)

circus house [1900s-1930s] (US Black)

coupling house [18C-19C]

creep joint [1920s+]

crib house [1910s-40s]

crib joint [1920s-40s]

fancy house [19C]
fast house [mid-19C-1940s] (US)
flash house [mid-late 19C]
flash-panny [mid-19C]
franzy house [20C] (US)
garden house [19C]
gay house [18C-1900s]
gingering joint [1940s+] (Aus.)
goat house [mid-19C]
goosing slum [mid-late 19C; 1950s] (US)
grind joint/house (US) [1960s+]
grinding-house [19C]
hook house [late 19C+] (US)
house in the suburbs [late 16C-late 17C]
house of civil reception [late 18C]
house of sale [late 16C-early 17C]
hump house [1920s] (US)
Irish clubhouse [1960s] (US gay)
jay house [late 19C-1900s] (US)
jazz house [1920s] (US; lit. 'fuck house')
joint [20C] (orig. US)
joy house [1910s-70s] (US)
jump joint [1930s+] (US)
knock shop [1960s+] (Aus.)
knocking-house [mid-late 19C; 1960s+]
knocking-joint [mid-late 19C; 1960s+]
ladies' boarding house [mid-19C-1900s]
leaning house [1970s+] (US Black)
leaping house [18C]
meat house [late 19C-1960s]
moll house [18C]

mollyhouse [early 18C-late 19C]
mot-house [mid-late 19C]
nanny house [late 17C-early 19C]
nautch house [late 19C-1940s] (US)
nookie house [1980s] (US)
notch house [1910s-70s] (US)
nugging house/ken [late 17C-early 19C]
occupying house [16C]
parlor house [mid-19C-1900s] (US)
peg-house [1940s+]
premises [19C]
punch house [late 17C-mid-19C]
rib joint [1940s+] (US)
rum ken [early-mid-19C] (UK Und.)
showhouse [20C]
slaughterhouse [1920s+]
slut hut [1980s+] (US gay)
smuggling-ken [late 18C-early 19C]
snoozing/snooze ken [early-mid-19C]
sport-house [20C] (W.I.)
sporting house [late 19C-1940s] (US)
tomcat house [1920s+]
toss parlour [1990s]
touch crib [19C]
trick house [1940s+] (US Black)
trugging house/ken [16C]
trugging place [16C]
vaulting house [late 16C-late 18C]
victualling-house [late 16C-early 17C]
warm shop/show [1910s-20s]

THE 'SHOP'

banging-shop [1960s-70s] (US)
blacksmith's shop [20C] ('where men are banging')
bumshop [mid-19C-1900s]
buttocking shop [19C]
buttonhole factory [19C]
cake shop [1910s+] (Aus.)
cat-shop [1930s-50s] (US)
cunt-shop [19C]
doll shop (US) [1980s]
fish market [mid-19C-1900s]
flesh market [mid-19C]
flesh-brokery [late 17C-18C]
flesh-shambles [early 17C]
girl-shop [late 19C]
greengrocery [mid-19C]
grinding-shop [19C]
hook shop [mid-19C+]
hotel-de-loose [late 19C] (US; plays on *de luxe*)
knocking-shop [mid-late 19C; 1960s+]
meat-works [1940s] (Aus.)
moll/molly shop [20C]
nanny shop [mid-19C]
whore shop [late 19C+]

THE 'SCHOOL'

academy [18C-early 19C]
cavaulting school [late 17C-early 19C] (lit. 'riding school')
dancing academy [18C] (*dance* = copulate)

finishing academy [18C]
ladies' college [18C]
pushing school [late 17C-19C]
vaulting school [late 16C-late 18C]

THE 'RANCH'

chicken ranch [1960s+]
gooseberry ranch [1930s-70s] (US)
goosing ranch [1920s-30s] (US)
hog ranch [late 19C+] (US)

THE PIMP

275

abbot on the cross [19C]
apple squire [16C-18C]
apple-monger [18C]
apron knight [16C]
apron squire [16C]
beard-jammer [1920s+] (US)
bellswagger/belswagger [late 16C-early 19C]
big daddy [1960s] (US)
bludgeoner [mid-19C]
bludger [late 19C+] (Aus.)
brother of the gusset [late 17C-19C]
c.p. [1920s] (abbr. *cunt-p*ensioner)
candyman [late 19C+] (US Black)
cash carrier [mid-late 19C]
cock-bawd [17C-early 19C]

cock-pimp [late 17C-late 18C]

cunt-pensioner [19C]

dona jack [late 19C-1900s]

easy rider [20C] (US Black)

faggot-master [19C]

faggoteer [19C]

faggoter [1960s+] (US Black; a pimp who sells the services
     of gay male prostitutes)

fancy cove [19C]

fancy Joseph [19C]

flashman [late 18C-late 19C]

fleshmonger [early-mid-17C]

fucker [mid-19C-1900s]

gamer [1960s-70s] (US Black)

gap-stopper [18C]

gorilla pimp [1960s+] (US Black; a pimp who controls
     prostitutes through threats and actual violence)

Haymarket hector [19C] (*Haymarket*, a brothel area
     of London; *hector* = a thug)

holemonger [19C]

holer [19C]

hoon (Aus./N.Z.) [1930s+]

hustler [1910s+] (Und.)

Iceberg Slim [1960s] (US Black; the pseudonym of
     real-life pimp Robert Beck)

jack-gagger [19C] (US)

jelly bean [1910s+] (US)

jock-gagger [early 19C]

knight of the gusset [19C]

led captain [17C-mid-19C]

lowrider [1930s+] (US Black)

macaroni [1960s+] (US)
mack [late 19C+] (US Und.)
mack man [1950s+] (US Black)
mackerel [1930s+] (US Und.)
mutton-tugger [late 16C-early 17C]
nookie bookie [1940s+] (US)
old man [1950s+] (US)
p [1920s-30s] (i.e. 'pimp')
pensioner to the petticoat [18C-19C]
petticoat merchant [19C+]
pimp [17C]

THE PIMP IN RHYMING SLANG

rhyming with *ponce*
   alphonse [1950s+]
   candle/candle-sconce [1920s+]
   charlie ronce [1930s+]
   ronson [1950s] (rhy. sl. rons[on] = ponce)
rhyming with *pimp*
   fish and shrimp [mid-20C]
   MacGimp/McGimp/magimp [1950s-60s] (US)
rhyming with *hoon*
   blue moon [1970s+] (Aus.)
   dish ran away with the spoon [1970s+] (Aus.)
   egg and spoon [1970s+] (Aus.)
   silver spoon [1940s+] (Aus.)
   silvery moon [1970s+] (Aus.)
   terry toon [1970s+] (Aus.)

pimp whisk [late 17C-early 19C] (a first-rate pimp)
pinch-bottom [19C]
pinch-buttock [19C]
pinch-cunt [19C]
pippin-squire [mid-late 17C]
player [1950s+] (orig. US Black)
ponce [late 19C+]
pounce-shicer [19C]
red bob [1940s+] (Aus.)
red deener [1940s+] (Aus.)
red penny [1940s+] (Aus.)
red shilling [1940s+] (Aus.)
she-napper [late 17C-mid-19C]
shundicknick [late 19C-1930s] (Yiddish)
smell-smock [18C]
smock merchant [17C]
smock pensioner [18C]
squire of the body [17C]
squire of the gusset [19C]
squire of the petticoat [late 17C-18C]
squire of the placket [17C]
stallion [late 17C-18C] (UK Und.)
stick slinger [mid-19C] (Aus.)
stringer [1910s+] (US)
suburb roarer [late 16C-late 17C]
sugar pimp [1960s+] (i.e. one who uses persuasion
    rather than threats)
tug-mutton [17C]
twat-faker [1900-20s]
twat-masher [1900-20s]
victualler [late 16C-early 17C]

TO WORK AS A PIMP

bird dog [1950s+] (US)
cop and blow [1950s-60s] (US Black)
mack [late 19C+]
offer out [1980s+]
ponce [1930s+]
push ponies [1960s+]
rig a jig [1970s] (US Black)
sawney [mid-19C]
sport [1980s+] (US Black)
talk game [1970s+] (US)
turn an honest penny [1910s-20s]
work from a book [1940s+] (US Black)

279

THE PIMP'S WOMEN

bottom woman [1950s-60s] (US Black; the most reliable
    woman in the pimp's 'stable')
corral [1960s-70s]
family [1950s-60s] (US Black)
flock [1930s+] (US)
horse [1920s+] (US; i.e. a prostitute in the pimp's 'stable')
lady [1970s+] (US)
main bitch [1940s+] (US Black; the pimp's favourite)
nest [1960s+] (US)
share certificate [1960s+] (US; the pimp's favourite)
sister-in-law [1940s+] (US Black; any prostitute other than
    the pimp's favourite)
stable [1930s+] (US)
star of the line [1960s+] (US Black; the pimp's favourite)

stomp-down woman [1960s-70s] (US Black; the hardest
   working woman in the pimp's 'stable')
string [1910s+] (US)
string of ponies [1910s+] (US)
top woman [1940s+] (the pimp's favourite)
wife [1940s+] (US Black; the pimp's favourite)
wife-in-law [1940s+] (US Black; any prostitute other than
   the pimp's favourite)

THE BASIC CLIENT

gonk [1960s]
john [late 19C+]
score [1960s+] (orig. US)
straight trick [1960s+]
trade [1930s+]
trick (orig. US) [1910s+]

THE SPECIALIST CLIENT

all-nighter [late 19C+] (a client who pays for a whole
    night's sex)
beat [1970s] (a client who likes to be beaten)
beer bottle beat [1970s] (US; a client who likes to be
    beaten with a beer bottle)
butt-plunger [1970s] (US; a client who inserts a dildo into
    his own anus and then walks around naked while the
    prostitute looks on)
champagne trick [1960sa+] (US; a particularly wealthy
    or generous client for a prostitute)
cream puff freak [1960s+] (US; a client who achieves sexual
    arousal by throwing gooey cakes at the prostitute)
dress-up [1970s] (a client who enjoys dressing up, usu. in
    the whore's clothes and make-up)
facial [1970s+] (a client who likes the woman to sit on his
    face, sometimes after she has inserted a suppository or
    even when she is having intercourse with another man)
freak/freak fuck [1960s+] (orig. US Black; a client who
    demands unusual or possibly physically dangerous services
    from a prostitute)
leapfrog [1970s] (a client who hires a number of prostitutes
    to play leapfrog while he watches)
live one [late 19C+] (US; a generous rich client)
looker [1970s] (orig. US; a client who wishes only to look
    at a prostitute, who is usu. naked, and occas. fondle her
    breasts)
needle freak [1970s+] (a sadistic client who derives pleasure
    from hiring a woman with large breasts and paying her for
    every needle she permits him to stick into her flesh)

no freak [1970s] (a client who wishes a prostitute to simulate
the role of a rape victim)

phone freak [1970s+] (a client who arranges to phone up a
prostitute and listen while she runs through a pornographic
monologue and he masturbates)

rabbit [1960s+] (a client who ejaculates quickly and thus
leaves the prostitute free to carry on her trade)

sniffer [1970s] (a client who enjoys sniffing the prostitute's
used underwear)

special [1970s+] (a client who has any particular tastes,
costumes, bondage, fetishes etc.)

talker [1970s+] (a client who wishes only to talk, either of sex
or merely of his life)

tin soldier [1970s+] (a client, usu. middle- or upper-class,
who doesn't want sex but only to act as a servant or 'slave'
to the prostitute)

word freak [1960s+] (a client who wishes the prostitute to
speak in obscenities for his sexual gratification)

Paying for It

SYPHILIS

bube [late 18C] (*bubo* = venereal swelling)
copper pox [1920s-1930s] (from the folk belief that were
    one to hold two copper coins beneath one's tongue during
    intercourse, one's partner would be infected with syphilis)
Cupid's measles [1940s-50s] (US)
deuce [17C+]
grincome [17C]
measles [mid-19C]
the old dog [1930s-50s] (US)
old joe [1910s+] (US)
pintle-blossom [18C-1900s] (a venereal bubo)
pox [16C+]
scabbado [17C]
syph [late 19C+]
sypho [1910s+]
    (Aus.)

Cupid's measles

THE PENALTIES OF TRAVEL

blow/knock with a French faggot-stick
[late 17C-early 18C] (refers to the loss of the
nose through the effects of syphilis)
French cannibal [early 17C]
French disease [late 16C-late 18C]
French marbles [late 16C]
French measles [early 17C]
French pig [late 17C-18C]
French pox [early 16C-late 18C]
the Frenchman [19C]
Naples canker [16C]
Neapolitan favour [16C]
Spanish gout [late 17C-early 19C]
Spanish needle [late 17C-early 19C]
Spanish pox [late 17C-18C]

GONORRHOEA

applause [1990s] (US Black; play on 'clap')
Barnwell ague [mid-17C-mid-19C]
blue balls [1930s+] (US)
botch [1960s] (US; lit. an eruptive sore)
bullhead clap [1940s-50s] (US; a very bad case of gonorrhoea)
clap [late 16C+] (Old Fr. *clapoir*, a venereal bubo)
clapper [mid-18C+] (US)
Covent Garden ague [17C-late 18C] (Covent Garden,
London, as a centre of whoring)

Cupid's itch [1930s+] (US)

double event [late 19C] (a simultaneous bout of syphilis
    and gonorrhoea)

drip [1960s+]

dripper [late 17C-18C]

Drury Lane ague [mid-18C-early 19C] (Drury Lane in
    London as a centre of whoring)

garden gout [early 19C] (i.e. Covent Garden, London)

gentleman's complaint [1920s+] (W.I.)

gleat/gleet [1940s+] (Aus.; lit. 'slime, purulent matter')

glue [late 19C]

goodyear [17C] (Fr. sl. *gouge*, a slut)

little casino [1960s+] (US; i.e. gonorrhoea as the 'lesser'
    form of VD)

nine-day blues [20C] (the incubation period for gonorrhoea)

running range [1920s-50s] (US Black; i.e. the discharge
    that accompanies gonorrhoea)

strain [1970s+] (US)

whites [19C] (the colour of the accompanying vaginal
    discharge)

THE VD CLINIC

blue-light clinic [20C] (Aus.)

clap clinic [20C]

dead lock [late 19C]

Mother Cornelius' tub [16C]

pickling tub [late 16C-18C]

powdering tub [late 16C-18C]

pox-hospital [1940s+]

propho [1910s+] (i.e. 'prophylaxis')

Venereal Disease in Rhyming Slang

rhyming with *siff*
    bang and biff [20C]
    will's whiff [20C]
rhyming with *pox*
    band in the box [1960s+]
    boots and socks [20C] (Aus.)
    cardboard box [1970s+]
    coachman on the box [20C]
    Collie Knox [1960s+]
    jack in the box [late 19C+]
    Nervo And Knox [1970s+]
    Reverend Ronald Knox [1950s]
    royal docks [20C]
    shoes and socks [20C]
    Surrey docks [1970s]
    Tilbury docks [late 19C+]
    Whitehaven docks [1970s]
rhyming with *clap*
    handicap [20C]
    horse and trap [1960s+]

Postscript: 'filthy' words

In October 1973, in what became a cause célèbre in the history of censorship, the US comedian George Carlin recorded a monologue in front of a live audience in a California theatre. He talked about 'the words you couldn't say on the public, uh, airwaves, um, the ones you definitely wouldn't say, ever'. The 12 words in question were:

fuck • motherfucker • shit • fart • piss • turd • cunt • cock • tits twat • cocksucker • ass

Following the broadcasting of the monologue by a New York radio station on 30 October 1973, a complaint was received by the Federal Communications Commission, which declared that the monologue, while not obscene, was certainly indecent and 'patently offensive'. The US Supreme Court later upheld this judgement. The 'Carlin twelve' thus entered into history as the ultimate in 'filth' – a blacklist of lexical profanity from which the ears of middle America were to be protected.

In the late 1990s, attitudes have relaxed sufficiently for it to be quite possible – even probable – for the listener/viewer to hear at least half of Carlin's words uttered in a single random evening of TV viewing. We now offer, therefore, our own 12 words and phrases culled from the pages of *The Big Book of Filth*, the public use and explanation of which – even in the more permissive atmosphere of the approaching third millennium – should only be attempted with the most extreme circumspection:

docking • tossed salad • butt-plunger • facial • felch get some cold comfort • get some duke • gummer high Russian • scatting • sniffer • spit out of the window